International Aid and Private Schools for the Poor

NEW THINKING IN POLITICAL ECONOMY

Series Editor: Peter J. Boettke, *George Mason University, USA*

New Thinking in Political Economy aims to encourage scholarship in the intersection of the disciplines of politics, philosophy and economics. It has the ambitious purpose of reinvigorating political economy as a progressive force for understanding social and economic change.

The series is an important forum for the publication of new work analysing the social world from a multidisciplinary perspective. With increased specialization (and professionalization) within universities, interdisciplinary work has become increasingly uncommon. Indeed, during the 20th century, the process of disciplinary specialization reduced the intersection between economics, philosophy and politics and impoverished our understanding of society. Modern economics in particular has become increasingly mathematical and largely ignores the role of institutions and the contribution of moral philosophy and politics.

New Thinking in Political Economy will stimulate new work that combines technical knowledge provided by the 'dismal science' and the wisdom gleaned from the serious study of the 'worldly philosophy'. The series will reinvigorate our understanding of the social world by encouraging a multidisciplinary approach to the challenges confronting society in the new century.

Recent titles in the series include:

International Aid and Private Schools for the Poor

Smiles, Miracles and Markets

Pauline Dixon

Senior Lecturer in International Development and Education, Newcastle University, UK

NEW THINKING IN POLITICAL ECONOMY

Edward Elgar
Cheltenham, UK • Northampton, MA, USA

Published by
Edward Elgar Publishing Limited
The Lypiatts
15 Lansdown Road
Cheltenham
Glos GL50 2JA
UK

Edward Elgar Publishing, Inc.
William Pratt House
9 Dewey Court
Northampton
Massachusetts 01060
USA

A catalogue record for this book
is available from the British Library

Library of Congress Control Number: 2012952658

This book is available electronically in the ElgarOnline.com
Economics Subject Collection, E-ISBN 978 1 78195 345 7

ISBN 978 1 78195 344 0 (cased)

Typeset by Servis Filmsetting Ltd, Stockport, Cheshire
Printed by MPG PRINTGROUP, UK

To Alison and Jackie
with all my love

Contents

About the author

Pauline Dixon is Senior Lecturer in International Development and Education at Newcastle University in the North East of England. She is Research Director of the E.G. West Centre at the University and Degree Programme Director of the Masters in International Development and Education. She lectures in economics, education policy and quantitative methods. Dr Dixon was International Research Coordinator on the John Templeton Project from 2003–2005, the Orient Global Project from 2007–2009 and is currently Research Director on research looking at education in conflict zones. She has around 40 publications, via academic journals, monographs and book chapters. She works as an advisor and external researcher with a number of companies including the English-based international charity Absolute Return for Kids (ARK) in Delhi, India. She has been instrumental in the setting up of an education voucher programme in the slums of Delhi and carrying out a randomised control trial to determine the effects on student outcomes. She is interested in the use of synthetic phonics in both government and low-cost private schools in India. Her passion is also identifying and nurturing gifted and talented children who live in slum areas around the world.

Preface – a vignette from Hyderabad

In 2000 I landed at Mumbai airport to transfer on to Hyderabad in the south. It was about 3a.m. They played some Andrew Lloyd Webber music on the plane as we'd disembarked. I was totally disappointed. I'd arrived for my first trip to India and had done so to a tune from *Cats*. Surely a sitar and tanpura would have been more fitting? Where was Ravi Shankar when you needed him? Air France was totally not getting it.

I wouldn't be disappointed for long. The transfer from the international to domestic terminal by charabanc bus was an experience in itself. Scared out of my wits, I teamed up with a young girl who had travelled from her home in Hounslow, West London. Indian parents but had never been to India herself. A typical *Bend it Like Beckham* moment. Together we managed to break free from hordes of beggars advising us that we were making a big mistake and getting on the wrong bus. If we didn't go with them we'd miss our flights, they warned. Poppycock!

Somehow we made it, bags and all, and the rest of the journey was without incident. This trip was to be the first of many for me over the next 12 years to a vibrant, entrepreneurial, pungent, exciting and enchanting India.

The next day, having been picked up from the Viceroy Hotel, and from the back of a moped, I noticed private schools everywhere. They are difficult to ignore. In the Old City of Hyderabad I saw them advertised on the back of auto rickshaws, signboards by the side of the road and on the roofs of the school buildings themselves. Children were walking to school or sitting in a row on their fathers' motorbikes, sometimes in threes and fours. They were carrying the biggest bags you've ever seen, with all the books they needed for the day. Uniforms so smart, I wondered how they ever kept them clean in such heat and grime of the city. Great school names stood out like 'Oxford Grammar School', 'Madina Mission', 'Genius High School', 'St Angels', 'Glossy Mission', 'New Bluebirds Grammar', 'St John's'. These private schools aren't for the rich, but the poor. This is the low-income side of town. Thousands of fee-paying affordable private schools are being run as businesses by entrepreneurs from within the community. Driving down one lane takes you by three, four, five private schools or more.

Holding my laptop in one arm and with the other wrapped around the waist of my moped driver, we bumped over potholes, missed other road users by inches, avoided cows, and got boomed at from behind by lorries the size of double-decker buses. Eventually zigzagging down the back lanes away from the noise we parked the bike outside Dawn High School.

My first private school visit was with Mr Khurrum, tall, handsome, with perfect manners and smile. I was invited to sit in his office to sip black tea with him. He welcomed me warmly. The ayah brought in snacks and more tea. In Hyderabad everyone seems to have more hours in the day, exuding a calm sedentary style in a hubbub of chaos.

After some time we appeared from behind the curtain hung at his office doorway like some actors in a play. The children greeted me warmly, some looked no more than three years old and were presenting me with flowers; others shook my hand and could have been 16. The school caters for children of all ages, known as a through school; most private schools are in Hyderabad. Calling on every classroom seems a must. No one wants to miss out on the attentions of a foreign visitor. The classrooms have no doors, just a doorway. No windows, just a space where a window could be. In each room a blackboard, chairs; children tightly packed in rows stand bolt upright to wish me 'good mor-ning ma-dam'. I ask each time what the lesson is – Telugu, Urdu, maths, social science, English, science – the teachers were so dedicated and most noticeably so were the children.

It was time to leave Mr Khurrum, but over the years I was destined to return many times, spending two wonderful birthdays at Dawn High School a decade apart!

But then it was off to a government school. I'm now getting my balance better on the back of the bike and even encourage direct right turns into the oncoming traffic. Saves time. We park up. Some children were wandering around in the playground and almost all the rooms were empty of children and teachers. However one was packed with about 60 children. The teacher was sitting at her desk. The children undertaking something on their own sitting on the floor, which was wet in some places and surrounded by buzzing mosquitoes. The children looked miserable and were obviously of different ages. I asked the teacher what they were doing and why there were so many in this class when the others seemed empty. She told me that the other teachers at the school were off. She was the only one present. Therefore she had all the children in one class. What were they doing? Math. The curriculum set out that the children should know the numbers from one to 10,000. So that's what they were doing. All term. Writing down the numbers each day from where they left off the day before: 899, 900, 901, 902, 903, 904, etc., etc., etc.

From that day forward these children became my motivation.

Introduction – never assume

Why is it so often assumed that the state should supply, finance and regulate schooling not only in developed, but developing countries? Arguments around equality of opportunity, positive externalities, the protection of minors, public and merit goods, social cohesion, democracy and the reduction of crime are all reasons advocated for state provision of education. This book does not set out all the economic arguments and counter-arguments as this has been done well elsewhere.[1]

What this book does do is question the role of the state by looking at the de facto privatisation of schooling in India. It also considers whether international aid agencies could effectively contribute to further the achievements of this incredible schools' market success story.

Until quite recently in many developing countries it had been assumed that school provision was virtually, and should be, a state provided monopoly. Not only supported by national governments but international aid agencies alike; pouring money into state education, however stagnant and ineffective, was the order of the day.

Billions of international aid agency dollars have been put into state schooling in Africa and India with very little or no effect. Monies targeting the poorest through bilateral aid have often become the victim of corruption and waste, ending up not being spent on schooling or education but in some corrupt official's bank account. Abolishing user fees has been the main quest of agencies such as UNESCO (United Nations Educational, Scientific and Cultural Organization), with the target of 'Education for All' having clouded the need for quality rather than quantity. This book explores why.

In India, the state school system that exists today was put in place during the days of the British Raj in order for a supposedly superior schooling model, mimicking that being proposed in England, to be replicated. This was the case irrespective of what already existed in the Indian context, that is a burgeoning indigenous private school market, and, as it happens, such a system was already working in Britain too. Chapter 1 explores these issues, considering aspects surrounding the establishment of schools built on the British model in India and the history and evidence that surrounded that execution. Census and survey documents of the day are scrutinised which provide evidence that supports Gandhi's declaration that the British uprooted the 'beautiful tree' of indigenous Indian education.

Running parallel to the Indian 'uprooting' was the implementation of state-provided and funded schools in England, initiated to 'fill the gaps' in private provision. E.G. West's work was the first to challenge the role of the state in education, providing historical evidence showing a burgeoning private sector in England and Wales before the state became involved initially through funding and then provision. Both the Indian and English cases will be considered in Chapter 1 as the two are inextricably linked.

International aid agencies have long been fascinated with education. Typically this focus has been on providing money to developing country governments, through bilateral and multilateral aid, in order to support fee free schooling for all and in recent years targeting the education millennium development goals. However, owing in part to my work with James Tooley and our research teams around the world, times may be changing, whether this is for the better remains to be seen. Chapter 2 sets out some of the recent thinking around whether or not providing developing country governments with aid can actually alleviate poverty and, specifically for our purpose, improve the quantity and quality of education and schooling. Evidence is scrutinised in order to provide a debate later in the book as to what kind of aid, and the best mechanisms to direct this aid, could promote and improve schooling in developing countries.

This book gives an account of what is currently happening on the ground in India with regard to schooling. That is, parents voting with their feet, sending their children to low-cost, entrepreneurially run, profit-making, private unaided schools. The most recent research with regard to schooling for the poor in India is explored in Chapter 3. Survey and census data are presented, as are comparisons between different school management types with regard to pupil achievement, teacher absenteeism and attendance, and facilities. Empirical research has shown a high proliferation of private unaided schools for the poor in India, this chapter summarises the evidence.

Now more than ever the spotlight, owing to the empirical evidence gathered over the last decade or so, has been shone on the affordable private unaided school sector. With aid agencies under pressure to deliver something meaningful, which shows positive results, the private school space has now captured the imagination and attention of bureaucrats. Chapter 4 sets out some possible ways international aid could be channelled in order to contribute to the continued success of private schools for the poor. The message, however, is that care is needed in order that the market process is not impeded or misdirected yet again. The interventions need to utilise frameworks that have been shown to be successful. All projects need to be evaluated through the use of randomised control trials or other valid research techniques to identify any effects of the interventions. A cost–benefit analysis should be undertaken for all projects in order to ascertain value for money, value added, sustainability and the possibility of the scalability of the intervention. Therefore Chapter 4 sets out recommendations for international aid agencies given the current evidence surrounding alternative strategies.

The final chapter brings the whole book together, providing not only a summary but a discussion of the way forward, offering a warning to those who wish to jump on the educational horse that is once again galloping in India and the dangers of the market losing hold of the reins yet again.

NOTE

1. See West (1965).

Acknowledgements

There are so many people I would like to thank, and without whom this book could not have been written. First, I'd like to mention those special school entrepreneurs in India, their pupils and teachers; most of all my dearest friends Fazalur Khurrum, Reshma Lohia, Mr Wajid, Mr Parvees, Mr Sajid and Khan Lateef Kahn. You and your children will remain in my heart always. You are the reason for my work.

The research upon which much of this book is based would not have taken place without funding from the Sir John Templeton Foundation. The opportunity the foundation gave was where this really all began for me. So thanks particularly to Charles Harper and Arthur Schwarz. Another big step was through my work with Absolute Return for Kids (ARK). A special mention goes to Paul Marshall, who had faith and still does – something about blowing the bloody doors off I remember. Also to Dame Sally Morgan who was there in Delhi and Lord Nat Wei who wasn't but had belief, along with Amitav Virmani, Leena Patel and Rasika Sirdar who worked determinedly with me in Delhi to make things work. And boy they did. Also in India, to my friends Gurcharan Das, Parth Shah, Barun Mitra, S.V. Gomathi, Aishwarya Ravindran, Baladevan Rangaraju, and Deepak and Barbara Lal who were all never far away.

Those who have inspired me include Pete Boettke, Israel Kirzner, Colin Riordan, Erik Gregory, Patrick Wolf, Brian Snowdon, Richard Graham, Mark Pennington, Philip Walling and Steven Pfeiffer. Thank you.

Finally to my dearest friends here at home, a special mention to Tom and Louise Kirkwood without whom I would never have made it, along with Jonathan and Katherine Clark and you all know why. Thanks also go to John and Anne-Marie Trevelyan for providing a home, to Steve Hardman and his family for improving it and to Chris and Janet Dickson for giving me freedom when I needed it. Also to Scott Miller, Lisa and Syd (with a y) Ahomet for keeping my body in shape when my mind was going and my treasured friends Louise Collyer and Jane Eggleston from Newcastle just for being there. Bless you. I also appreciate the support of my students and colleagues at Newcastle University, especially Charles Harvey, Simon Kometa, Rene Koglbauer, James Stanfield, James Tooley, Chris Counihan, Michael Burgess, Geoff Calder, Carl Towler and Gerry Docherty. My deepest of thanks to both Chloe Mitchell and Alison Hornbeck of Edward Elgar Publishing for all of their help and correspondence in preparing this manuscript.

But most of all to my twin sister, Jackie, and Mum, Alison, who always had faith and knew I could do it and were always by my side, even when things got tough. I would be nothing without you. This book is dedicated to you both with much love.

Abbreviations

AFED	Association for Formidable Educational Development
AP	Andhra Pradesh
APF	Azim Premji Foundation
APPEP	Andhra Pradesh Primary Education Project
APRESt	Andhra Pradesh Randomized Evaluation Study
ARK	Absolute Return for Kids
ASER	Assessment Survey Evaluation Research (impact in Hindustani)
BDH	Bono de Desarrollo Humano
BPL	Below Poverty Line
CCT	Conditional Cash Transfer
CESSP	Cambodia Education Sector Support Project
CfBT	Centre for British Teachers
DAC	Development Assistance Committee
DEO	District Education Officer
DfID	Department for International Development
DPEP	District Primary Education Programme
EC	European Commission
ENABLE	Ensure Access to Better Learning Experiences
EVS	Education Voucher Scheme
FSSAP	Female Secondary School Assistance Program
G	Government schools
GDP	Gross Domestic Product
GGV	Gray Ghost Ventures
GMC	Gray Matters Capital
GNI	Gross National Income
GOAP	Government of Andhra Pradesh
GOI	Government of India
GRS-S	Gifted Rating Scale-School Form
IADB	Inter American Development Bank
IBRD	International Bank for Reconstruction and Development
IDA	International Development Association
IFAD	International Fund for Agricultural Development
IFC	International Finance Corporation

ISFC	Indian School Finance Company
JFPR	Japan Fund for Poverty Reduction
JPS	Jaring Pengamanan Sosial
LEAPS	Learning and Educational Achievement in Pakistan Schools
M4P	Making Markets Work for the Poor
MDGs	Millennium Development Goals
MLA	Member of the Legislative Assembly
MLC	Member of the Legislative Council
MPCP	Milwaukee Parental Choice Program
MPI	Multidimensional Poverty Index
MPS	Mont Pelerin Society
NAPPS	National Association of Proprietors of Private Schools
NCERT	National Council of Educational Research and Training
NPE	National Policy on Education
OB	Operation Blackboard
ODA	Official Development Assistance
OECD	Organisation for Economic Co-operation and Development
PA	Private aided schools
PACES	Programa de Ampliación de Cobertura de la Educación Secundaria
PEF	Punjab Education Fund
POA	Programme of Action
PPP	Purchasing Power Parity
PROBE	Public Report on Basic Education in India
PUA	Private unaided schools
RCT	Randomised Control Trial
RMSA	Rashtriya Madhyamik Shiksha Abhiyan
RTE	Right to Education Act
SAT	Sinapi Aba Trust
SDC	Swiss Agency for Development and Cooperation
SIDA	Swedish International Development Cooperation Agency
SIVP	School Improvement Voucher Program
SPEIP	Support to Private Education Institution Programme
SRC	School Report Card
SSA	Sarva Shiksha Abhiyan
TIMSS	Trends in International Mathematics and Science Study
UN	United Nations
UNDP	United Nations Development Programme
UNESCO	United Nations Educational, Scientific and Cultural Organization
UNICEF	United Nations Children's Fund
UP	Uttar Pradesh

1 Jumping onto the galloping horses – even in India

The first major work to challenge the role of governments in education was E.G. West's *Education and the State*, published in 1965 by the Institute of Economic Affairs (IEA). West was the first to really question the accepted wisdom of the role of the state by looking back into British and US history.

At the first meeting of the Mont Pelerin Society (MPS) in 1947 a group of 39 liberals, made up of economists, philosophers, historians, political scientists and jurists, discussed a range of potentially damaging issues that were threatening Western liberal civilisation. Friedrich A. Hayek, one of the leading free market and Austrian economists who had gained acclaim owing to his 1944 publication *Road to Serfdom*, invited the 39 to the first meeting. The group highlighted six main aims of the MPS with a central issue of 'combating the misuse of history for the furtherance of creeds hostile to liberty'.[1] Indeed four years later the 1951 MPS meeting solely focused on how opponents of capitalism, such as Marx and Engels, had distorted the history of capitalism in the industrial revolution in Britain and the US. According to Hayek, historical facts were being misrepresented in order for the socialist cause to be strengthened. It was important for work to be done by the members of the MPS, along with others, to seek out the true facts and overturn some historical fallacies. West attended his first MPS meeting in 1962 and was to be influenced by MPS founders and members, primarily Milton Friedman but also James Buchanan and Gordon Tullock. Milton Friedman had already suggested the use of education vouchers in 1955, and Friedman and West entered into some lengthy discussions regarding education and the role of the state. As for Buchanan and Tullock, they were the founding figures of public choice theory, predicting the behaviour of government bureaucracies, recognising that politicians are self-interested utility maximising individuals. And in that case their political decisions may not necessarily represent what is best for the public good, but their own self-interest; 'the political machinery is seen, in fact, largely as operated by interest groups, vote-maximising politicians and self-seeking bureaucracies'.[2] West also was deeply taken with Hayek's concern regarding historical fallacies and the way history was being used by socialists to forward their ideas and policies.

The second part of this chapter will summarise West's thesis and findings with regard to education in England before the state began to fund and provide schools. The central argument being that there is a gross misunderstanding of historical fact with regard to schooling prior to state involvement and provision of schools. In fact, before state intervention there was a flourishing private schooling system that catered for the poor as well as the rich. This is still relatively unknown owing to a misguiding and misinterpretation of historical artefacts, data and records. However, the evidence from West's work is presented here to try to rectify some of these misconceptions.

What West would have been excited about is the de facto privatisation of schooling in India and other developing countries. He did not really live long enough to appreciate all the empirical work and research that was about to be undertaken. West died just weeks before he was to attend a lecture given in his honour planned to take place at Newcastle University in 2001. What was about to be uncovered in the years after his death mirrored the historical discoveries of West's own research. So not only were West's hypotheses borne out by historical evidence but what was found in the slums and low-income areas of India mirrored what had been occurring in England in the early nineteenth century.

West also did not know about the British 'uprooting the beautiful tree' of India's indigenous education system in the early 1800s. Census and survey data gathered by Sir Thomas Munro, who became the governor of the Madras Presidency in 1819, provide evidence to show the destruction of all that was good with regard to education at that time. The first part of this chapter looks at this evidence and its implications, showing inextricably linked historical episodes of private schools' markets being replaced by a publically provided and run monopoly.

BEFORE THE RAJ – THE INDIA EXPERIENCE

Uprooting the Beautiful Tree

On 20 October 1931, during a three-month stay in England, Mahatma Gandhi gave a talk at Chatham House, London. Here he revealed something interesting:

> I say without fear of my figures being challenged successfully, that today India is more illiterate than it was fifty or a hundred years ago, and so is Burma, because the British administrators, when they came to India, instead of taking hold of things as they were, began to root them out. They scratched the soil and began to look at the root, and left the root like that, and the beautiful tree perished.[3]

Fascinating in itself, claiming that the British had come to India and started to destroy an already flourishing indigenous education system. He continued:

> The village schools were not good enough for the British administrator, so he came out with his programme. Every school must have so much paraphernalia, building, and so forth.[4]

According to Gandhi, the British came with their 'expensive' and overly prescriptive state-funded, state-provided, state-regulated system where a school was only deemed functional if it provided certain facilities, most of which may not have contributed to quality and in fact were alien to the surroundings of nineteenth-century India. Gandhi claimed there were data, gathered by Sir Thomas Munro, to show operational unrecognised (unregulated) private schools prior to any British intervention:

> There are statistics left by a British administrator which show that, in places where they have carried out a survey, ancient schools have gone by the board, because there was no recognition for these schools, and the schools established after the European pattern were too expensive for the people, and therefore they could not possibly overtake the thing.[5]

So Gandhi believed that owing to the implementation of a state schooling system in India, by the British, the population was now more illiterate than before. Offering schools funded, provided and regulated by the state was an expensive method that India could not afford. The indigenous schooling system, which was successfully educating children in the villages of India, was destroyed by the British:

> I defy anybody to fulfil a programme of compulsory primary education of these masses inside of a century. This very poor country of mine is ill able to sustain such an expensive method of education. Our state would revive the old village schoolmaster and dot every village with a school both for boys and girls.[6]

So on what evidence was Gandhi basing his claims? How many such schools were there? How were they funded? And, what quality of education did they provide for those who accessed them?

Indigenous Education in Nineteenth-Century India – Quantity

In the summer of 1822 a survey and census of education in India was initiated by 'Munro's Minute', also known as a memorandum entitled 'Ordering the Collection of Detailed Information of Indigenous Education'.[7] Munro set out in the memorandum to make it clear that opinions regarding indigenous education were, up until then, built on 'mere conjectures of individuals unsupported by any authentic documents', and as such should be provided 'little attention'.[8] What Munro was suggesting was to undertake an education survey, similar to previous geographical and agricultural surveys carried out in the Madras Presidency, to find out more about the population and their 'resources'. According to Munro, in 1822 there was 'no record to show the actual state of education throughout the country'[9] and this proposed survey would 'enable us to form an estimate of the state of instructions among the people'.[10] In this regard Munro was asking the district collectors to make lists of schools in which reading and writing were taught. Within each of these schools, information was to be collected on the number of scholars attending, their caste, the books read, school timings, and 'the monthly or yearly charge to the scholars'.[11] Interestingly and importantly, Munro goes on to say towards the end of his memorandum that:

> it is not my intention to recommend any interface whatever in the native schools. Everything of this kind ought to be carefully avoided, and the people should be left to manage their schools in their own way.[12]

So just to be clear, Munro was requesting a survey of schooling. The intention was to have an official document that set out information that currently was not available. It was not the purpose to change, improve, take over or interfere with what was functioning already on the ground.

So what did the census and survey data show?

The data from 20 districts of the Madras Presidency took between one and three years to make its way back to Munro. Within those districts, 11,575 schools were located catering for 157,195 children.[13] Figures were also provided by some of the collectors who believed that many children were receiving education in their homes. Home schooling, Munro believed, was very common in the presidency. For example, the Collector of Madras discovered that there were five times more children educated in their homes than in school, the figures being 26,963 and 5699 respectively.

In March 1826 Munro produced a summary of the data, estimating that over one-third of male school-aged children was being educated, either in school or at home. It was more difficult to provide figures for girls, with the majority having been thought to receive education in the home rather than in school. What the evidence showed was that in India the number of children benefitting from education was 'higher than it was in most European countries'.[14] Not only did the education system cater for the elite, but it also catered for the poorest children (dalit or backward caste) making up in some districts around one-third of school enrolments.

Munro was not the only one to gather data on India's indigenous education. Another survey was carried out in the British Presidency of Bengal, the result of which was published in 1841 as the 'State of Education in Bengal 1835 to 1838' and became part of the documents known as the Adam Reports. The findings showed that there were 'some 100,000 such schools in Bengal and Bihar'[15] and that:

> the system of village schools is extensively prevalent; that the desire to give education to their male children must be deeply seated in the minds of parents even of the humblest classes; and that these are the institutions, closely interwoven as they are with the habits of the people and the customs of the country.[16]

The same was true in the Punjab and Bombay.

In the Presidency of Bombay it was documented by senior officials that 'there is hardly a village, great or small, throughout our territories, in which there is not at least one school, and in larger villages more'.[17] That is, private schools. The same was true for the Punjab.

Census data therefore from the Presidencies of Madras, Bombay, Bengal and the Punjab show a flourishing indigenous education system operating in India before the British replaced it. Children were being educated both in school and at home, some children remaining in education for 10–12 years.[18] The system was comparable to that which operated in European countries.

But who was paying for it and how much did it cost?

Indigenous Education in Nineteenth-Century India – Cost

Looking back at the data with regard to education funding supplied by 19 of the collectors of the Madras Presidency, 16 of the reports show that schooling was 100 per cent privately funded. The remaining three collectors provided data that show that around 98–99 per cent of schools were privately funded with only 1–2 per cent supported by the state.

Data collected from 630 private primary schools surveyed by one of the collectors shows that some private schools offered teaching in the local language, others in Persian and finally some in English. Only 15 of the 630 schools in his district did not charge fees. Fees seemed to differ depending upon the medium of instruction, with the English-medium schools charging the most. Of those teaching in the local language fees ranged from 15 annas[19] to 21 rupees per year (collected on a monthly basis), the fee-paying Persian schools charged between 14 annas and 24 rupees per year, and the English private schools from 7.5 rupees to 42 rupees per year. In general fees were charged relevant to the child's educational stage; the higher up the educational ladder one climbed the higher the fee. Also, poorer students were often charged a small proportion of the full fee. Evidence of such private school philanthropy or the giving of scholarships for the poor is set out in William Adam's report from Bengal 1835–1838:

> Another mode adopted in two instances, of regulating the fees is according to the means of the parents whose children are instructed; a half, a third, or a fourth less being charged to the children of poor than to the children of rich parents in the successive stages of instruction.[20]

And a letter to the board of revenue in 1825 from the 'Collector from Madras Cutcherry' (an L.G.K. Murray) also indicates that the poor pay less for their education:

> It will be observed that the schools now existing in the country are for the most part supported by the payments of the people who send their children to them for instruction. The rate of payment for each scholar varies in different districts and according to the different circumstance of the parents of the pupils, from 1 anna to 4 rupees per mensem, the ordinary rate among the poorer classes appears to be generally about 4 annas, and seldom to exceed 1/2 rupee.[21]

So if education existed and parents were able to pay for it why did the British want to replace it with something Gandhi regarded as unsustainable and inferior? What were the arguments they used to 'uproot' this beautiful tree?

Indigenous Education in Nineteenth-Century India – Sir Philip Hartog

Listening to Gandhi's talk at Chatham House was Sir Philip Hartog, founder of the School of Oriental Studies, University of London and ex-vice chancellor of the University of Dacca. He was positively fuming regarding Gandhi's claims and remarks. A lengthy debate was entered into, Hartog requesting Gandhi to revoke his comments. So incensed was Hartog that he gave a series of lectures to dismiss Gandhi's claims regarding the flourishing private system uprooted by the British. Hartog set out to question the data concerning both the quantity and quality of education available. His main aim was to dispel any doubt that may have been instigated by Gandhi's talk. He wanted to show that what the British had introduced provided more access and better quality than what existed previously.

Owing to what can only be described as Hartog's prejudices, the suggestion was that the original figures regarding the number of private schools and children attending school were exaggerated and inaccurate. So upon what foundation was Hartog basing his argument?

With regard to quantity, Hartog simply took the collectors' reports that suited his needs, dismissing the rest. It is relatively easy to dismiss Hartog's interpretation, therefore, of the data regarding the quantity of schooling, as it is all so well documented by Munro and the Adam Reports. Blatantly Hartog just used the data he found most fitting to bolster his argument, dismissing the rest as exaggerated. If Hartog were correct about an exaggeration, one would actually have to ask why individual collectors would inflate such figures. It was neither in their interest to over or under estimate the number of schools they found. It is easy to ascertain that Hartog only considered one or two of the collectors' reports in his presentation of the data to support his misguiding of historical fact.

But what about the quality of these schools? Was Hartog right to question the quality of the private schools? And was this so-called lack of quality a good enough reason for them to be replaced by a school system funded and provided by the state?

There are two ways to try to uncover what the quality of these low-cost private schools must have been like. First, parents, including poor parents, were paying for their children to be educated. If the quality of schooling or the education attained was so poor, as suggested by Hartog, then why were parents prepared to send their children for such a protracted amount of time and at such a cost? Parents would surely be acting rationally, as self-interested individuals. Hartog's attitude then dismisses the parents' ability to judge for themselves the benefits education brings, as well as the value judgements that go with the decision to send their children to gain an education rather than carry out some other activity. Therefore the rationality and self-interest of parents towards education seems to imply that the quality of 'schooling' for them at least was adequate.

Second, what about the written evidence surrounding quality? In the original census and survey carried out by Munro there had been no requirement to comment on the quality of the schools. Such judgements would anyway have been subjective as no testing was being carried out. However, six of the 20 collectors did provide comments on school quality. The majority of these comments were positive.

In a report from 29 October 1822, the assistant collector in charge at Seringapatam (an H. Vibart) noted that:

> the extent of information acquired under the present prevailing system of education is extremely limited – nothing more is professed to be taught in these day-schools than reading, writing, and arithmetic, just competent for the discharge of the common daily transactions of society.[22]

This actually could be taken as a positive comment; that is, reading, writing and arithmetic were competently taught and learnt, which would allow the children to participate in their communities and within society.

L.G.K. Murray, the collector from Madras, was very positive in his report of November 1822, stating in his fourth and fifth points that:

> it is generally admitted that before they attain their thirteenth year of age, their acquirement in the various branches of learning are uncommonly great, a circumstance very justly ascribed to an emulation and perseverance peculiar only to the Hindoo castes ... Astronomy, Astrology, etc., are in some instances taught to the children of the poorer class.[23]

In 1823, the North Arcot District Collector William Cooke commented that schooling also had a positive effect, allowing children to gain employment in different occupational circumstances:

> The Tamil, Taloogoo and Hindwy schools are the most extensive; to these the scholars are sent generally about the age of 5 and in the course of five or six years are generally found sufficiently forward to commence assisting in the preparation or copying of the accounts, according to their different walks in life, sometimes as volunteers in the public Cutcherries or in the situations with Curnums, Shroffs, Merchants or others, whence they graduate to situations in the public service or their hereditary occupations.[24]

Agreeing with Cooke, J.F. Lane, the collector from Masulipatam, in 1823 believed the children gained an education that also allowed them to take up placements in employment. Describing the pedagogy and the process thus:

> They are first taught to read the letters, spelling, and the names both common and proper, writing on the sand with their fingers. When they are perfect in that, they are taught the reading of books (Balaramayanum, Amram, etc.), on cadjans (useful for the boys) in Sanscrit and Gentoo as well as letters of correspondence, books of mathematics, accounts, etc., etc., according to the pleasure of the relations of the boys ... As soon as the boys have learnt to write well on cadjans or on paper they are removed from the schools to some of the public or private offices of curnums, paishcar, or to be improved in keeping accounts, or to schools of foreign languages such as Persian, English, etc.[25]

However the remaining two collectors, S. Smalley and A.D. Campbell were a little more critical:

> Few of the schoolmasters are acquainted with the grammar of the language, which they profess to teach, and neither the master nor scholars understand the meaning of the sentences, which they repeat ... Education cannot well, in a civilized state, be on a lower scale than it is and I much fear there does not exist the same desire for improvement as is reported of the natives of Bengal.[26]

However, Smalley does go on to note that there was no intention to 'interfere with the people in the mode of education'[27] and that the British were only considering providing some kind of aid to those private institutions that already existed.

So even though it is very difficult to ascertain from these few comments the true 'quality' of instruction that was actually taking place in the schools and homes at the time, it would seem fair to say that parents were satisfied, prepared to pay and allow their children to attend rather than carry out some other duty or role. Therefore the opportunity cost of sending one's child to school must have been such that it was of benefit not only to the child, but the family. The majority of the collectors who commented on quality had positive things to say. So it is difficult to ascertain from the reports why Hartog believed that the quality was poor and that the British needed to intervene to upgrade and improve the system. What was also pertinent was that within these reports it was made quite clear that the indigenous education should remain intact.

So if the quantity and quality proved to be adequate then what could Hartog hang his coat onto? Also highlighted by the Adam survey in Bengal were issues and details around teacher pay, buildings and pedagogy.

Regarding teacher remuneration, Adam believed that teachers in Bengal were paid a poor wage (owing to minimal fees paid by the parents) and therefore this must imply that the most engaging and appropriately qualified teachers were not being attracted to the profession:

> The teachers depend entirely upon their scholars for subsistence, and being little respected and poorly rewarded, there is no encouragement for persons of character, talent or learning to engage in the occupation.[28]

However, the pay teachers were receiving was not considered low at that time compared to other opportunities. It was just that Adam believed that teachers were entitled to receive an amount greater than that determined by the market:

> I have spoken of the emoluments of the teachers as low; but I would be understood to mean that they are low, not in comparison with their qualifications, or with the general rates of similar labour in the district, but with those emoluments to which competent men might be justly considered entitled.[29]

Not much wrong there then.

With regard to school buildings, the reports noted that education took place in a number of spaces including places of worship, private dwellings, in the open air and in other parts of the village. This implied that typically there was not one building exclusively utilised for the purpose of schooling, which according to Adam brought certain 'disadvantages'. But surely the fact that there were no purpose-built schools implied the efficient and effective use of space allowing for an affordable form of education?

Having teachers being paid the market rate and education being carried out utilising other buildings or appropriate spaces should be considered a good thing?

And how about pedagogy then, could Hartog be onto something there? The Adam Reports urged generally that teaching methods used in the private schools should be 'abandoned'.[30] But oddly enough they state that they better equip the scholars with the skills needed to participate within society than schools in Scotland! So why replace the methods if superior to that in Britain?

Other reports from Bombay talk about the simplicity, effectiveness, as well as the economy, of learning in the private schools;[31] commending methods that lead to the ability for the learner to be accurate, competent, clear and concise. Peer teaching was used extensively throughout India, where the 'Master' relays knowledge to the older or brighter students who in turn communicate the information to the younger or less capable children who are learning in groups. This method had been observed and catalogued in India from as early as 1623 by Peter Della Valle[32] and was regarded as an effective 'wisdom of crowds' type pedagogy. Indeed, so good was the method of peer teaching that when Dr Andrew Bell encountered it in 1787 he copied the idea and brought the method back to England some ten years later. Bell published a description of the 'Madras Method' as he called it upon his return to England and the system was adopted in British schools, including the Lancasterian schools created by Joseph Lancaster.

So why replace something that seemed to be working?

There was no doubting the quantity and (looking at the reports of the day) quality with regard to learning, effectiveness and efficiency, which seem more than adequate. Teacher pay was driven by market rates and education was regarded as something that could take place in a multitude of spaces without the need to build specific places of learning which would have been costly. Indeed, so successful were the pedagogical methods used in India, they were brought back to England to be implemented in British schools.

It would seem from the evidence that Hartog's dismissal of Gandhi's claims was more based on his own preference for education being centrally provided, funded and controlled as opposed to private and indigenous. Hartog would not be able to reconcile any thought that the British could have intervened if there were no reasons to. Hartog's manipulation of the historical facts during his presentations was misleading and misrepresentative. Whatever the reason for which the British 'uprooted the beautiful tree' of indigenous education in India, it was not because it was inadequate. As stated by Gandhi during his talk at Chatham House, irrespective of all of this evidence and irrespective of the promises not to intervene, the British were about to do exactly that. Munro, before the census collection, had stated that it was not his intention to interfere with what was found, allowing the schools to be managed in a way suitable to their context. At all costs any interference was to be 'carefully avoided'.[33]

Things were to change in 1835.

Thomas Babington Macaulay, the president of the General Committee of Public Instruction for the British Presidency, recommended 'uprooting the beautiful tree' and setting up a system of publically funded village schools. According to Macaulay, in 1835:

> The great object of the British Government ought to be the promotion of European literature and science among the natives of India, and that all the funds appropriated for the purposes of education would be best employed on English education alone.[34]

Macaulay was hugely dismissive of the private indigenous schools and the content being taught within the system. His recommendations and comments, irrespective of the work set out by Munro, the Adam Reports and others from Bombay, led in 1854 to the setting up of a state education system with state-funded teacher training, universities, the provision of funds for colleges and high schools, and funds that would bring the private schools under state control. It was something that Hartog defended and Gandhi vociferously challenged as too costly and unnecessary. The British introduced a system, when in fact they had sworn they would not, that crowded out indigenous education in India.

Little did Hartog and Gandhi know that in the new millennium parent power would be reversing imperialism, reclaiming education in order for the beautiful tree to begin again to be nurtured.

But what was happening in England around this time? Did a private schools system exist in parallel in the villages of Yorkshire and Northumberland just as it did in Madras, Bengal and the Punjab? Leaving the shores of India, where state education was just beginning, evidence was also being collected in England, just as in India, revealing an educated populace without the state.

EDUCATION AND THE STATE IN ENGLAND

E.G. West's *Education and the State* was first published in 1965. What West argues in the book is that before 1870, when the major state intervention into education in England and Wales began, school attendance and literacy rates were above 90 per cent. Obviously causing impassioned debate at the time, the book and its thesis were reviewed in several publications and newspapers, not only in developed countries, but discussions even reached India. According to the *Economic Times of India* on 31 January 1966, West's *Education and the State:*

> deserves to be read ... it is undoubtedly worthwhile for policy-makers, even in the socialistic political culture of India, to be aware of a line of argument which undoubtedly stems from a totally different historical situation.[35]

Interestingly, as is set out in this chapter, the evidence with regard to schooling in India prior to the British imposing a state system there shows that the assumption made by the *Economic Times of India* regarding a 'totally different historical situation' is misplaced. The historical situation with respect to schooling in India is actually inextricably linked to that in England and Wales. Another book review written in India concerning *Education and the State*, revealed among E.G. West's papers after his death, noted:

> At a time when the private sector in education in India is threatened with extinction ... Dr West furnishes a powerful armoury of arguments against Statism in education. Conditions in India differ radically from those in England, but to us as to those in that distant island the same choice between freedom and totalitarianism in education has been presented.[36]

So, as in the work of Dharampal above, how did E.G. West come to the assumptions he did? That is, that prior to state intervention in schooling in England and Wales, the USA and other countries education of the poor was met by the private sector without the support of the state. West looks at literacy rates (inferring the ability to read and write) and the quantity of schooling using quantitative evidence from parliamentary debates as well as anecdotal evidence from the period. Two main dates are important here; 1833 saw the first government subsidies to education, provided through taxation, and 1870 saw the Forster Act, which instigated the provision of Board Schools, funded partly by the state.

Literacy

Anecdotal evidence supports the thesis that literacy amongst the English population before the introduction of state-supported schooling was in fact high. With regard to literacy in the first 33 years of the nineteenth century, West states that 'the effect of state activity upon individual efforts to become literate was one of deliberate hindrance'.[37] What West believed the English government wanted to do was to prevent the spread of political literature among the poor. Therefore fiscal and legal action was taken against newspapers, especially those that were critical of government. At the time, Tom Paine's *Rights of Man* had sold one and a half million copies. Reading also took place in the home, with the Bible being read extensively, as well as popular literature and serialised fiction. The government felt that it needed to suppress the spread of some kinds of literature and therefore try to contain what the 'lower orders' were reading. To stifle the reading of such potentially damaging publications, public reading rooms were closed down and licences withdrawn from coffee houses, public houses and inns where certain newspapers were received and read.

What more formal data from the early nineteenth century show is that before the state became involved in education, schools taught children to read before they learnt to write. Learning to read at the time was considered more important as the need to write was quite limited, especially before the introduction of the penny post in 1840. Writing was also expensive owing to the taxes that were placed on writing materials. Reading therefore was the main focus of education.

Looking at the literacy rates amongst different sections of society, the data shows that a high proportion of people were literate. First, 87 per cent of children between the ages of nine and 16 years living in the workhouses of Norfolk and Suffolk in 1838 could read and 53 per cent could write.[38] Second, 79 per cent of miners in 1840 from Northumberland and Durham could read, with more than half being able to write.[39] Third, a report looking at education in 1839 in the borough of Kingston upon Hull found that out of 14,526 adults, 14,109 had attended a day or evening school and 92 per cent of all adults could read.[40] These adults would have been around 15 years old when the first government subsidies were introduced in schools in 1833. Most would have left school by the age of 11. Their ability to read was not fostered through government support but by non-government sources, mainly through parents paying fees for their children to be educated. By the 1860s it is believed that nine out of ten people in England could read. According to the figures, when the 1870 Board Schools (government schools) began to operate 93 per cent of school leavers were already literate. State intervention into schooling did

not instigate literacy. Literacy levels were already high. There was therefore no justification for the state to get involved in schooling with regard
to literacy levels amongst its citizens. The private and philanthropic educational institutions were already ensuring that the majority were literate.

Nineteenth-Century Private Schools in England

So prior to the introduction of Board Schools and the Forster Act of 1870,
93 per cent of school leavers were already literate. Government subsidies
to education started in 1833 and amounted to a total of £20,000 given
to just two voluntary school organisations, the National Society and the
British and Foreign School Society. In 1869, irrespective of almost 40
years of subsidy, 'two thirds of school expenditure was still coming from
voluntary sources, especially from the parents, directly or indirectly'.[41]
The remaining third would have come from taxation, which was more
burdensome on the working classes owing to its regressive nature.

In the early nineteenth century there were different private agencies
within which learning could take place. These included the Mechanics
Institute, the Literary and Philosophic Societies, Sunday schools as well as
tuition being carried out in the home. And there were also private schools,
deriving their income from privately paid fees without any degree of public
support. James Mill noted, in the *Edinburgh Review* of 1813, around the
period of the Napoleonic war:

> From observation and inquiry assiduously directed to that object, we can
> ourselves speak decidedly as to the rapid progress which the love of education
> is making among the lower orders in England. Even around London, in a circle
> of fifty miles radius, which is far from the most instructed and virtuous part of
> the kingdom, there is hardly a village that has not something of a school; and
> not many children of either sex who are not taught more or less reading and
> writing. We have met with families in which, for weeks together, not an article
> of sustenance but potatoes had been used; yet for every child the hard-earned
> sum was provided to send them to school.[42]

The number of children in school, funded by non-government means,
including parents paying fees, increased from around 478,000 in 1818 to
1,294,000 in 1834 without any input from the state. Henry Brougham, in
a speech to the House of Lords in May 1835, warned that owing to the
increase in schooling and the numbers of children attending, the government would need to take the 'greatest care' when interfering with it:

> [w]here we have such a number of schools and such means of education
> furnished by the parents themselves from their own earnings and by the
> contributions of well disposed individuals in aid of those whose earnings

were insufficient, it behoves us to take the greatest care how we interfere with a system which prospers so well of itself; to think well and long and anxiously, and with all circumspection and all foresight, before we thrust our hands into a machinery which is now in such a steady, constant, and rapid movement; for if we do so in the least degree incautiously, we may occasion ourselves no little mischief, and may stop that movement which it is our wish to accelerate.[43]

By 1851 there were 2,144,378 children in day schools. The 1851 census shows that 85 per cent of these were in private schools, that is, according to the census 'all schools which derive their income solely from (fee) payments or which are maintained with a view to pecuniary advantage'.[44] The remaining 15 per cent were attending schools that were 'supported in any degree' by the state and at that time this could have implied minimum support.

In 1858 the Newcastle Commission on Popular Education was set up to carry out a survey and census of schooling in England and Wales. Reporting in 1861 it showed a total of 2,535,462 children in school. Using an estimate of children being in school for 5.7 years, this implied that almost all children were in school. According to the report:

Wherever the Assistant Commissioners went, they found schools of some sort, and failed to discover any considerable number of children who did not attend school for some time, at some period in their lives.[45]

The report goes on to advise that the provision of schooling was such that there were no serious gaps in provision and therefore did not recommend the provision of state schools, but to improve the payment of direct grants to independent schools along with the inspection of private schools. According to West:

the general theme was the control and encouragement of the existing private framework rather than the political creation of new types of collectively organised schools.[46]

The commission reported:

The proportion of children receiving instruction to the whole population is, in our opinion, nearly as high as can be reasonably expected. In Prussia, where it is compulsory, it is 1 in 6.27; in England and Wales it is, as we have seen 1 in 7.7; in Holland it is 1 in 8.11; in France it is 1 in 9.0. The presence of this proportion of the population in school implies (as is shown by the foregoing calculations) that almost every one receives some amount of school education at some period or other ...[47]

It is interesting to note the similarities between the survey and census data from the Madras Presidency in India as stated in the Adam Reports compared with the Newcastle Commission's findings in England and Wales. Private schools provided an education for the majority of children. In both cases it was advised that the current status quo should not be meddled with and that the private sector be encouraged to expand. But just as Thomas Babington Macaulay was entering stage right, ignoring the entire plot of what had been shown by the survey and census data in India, enter stage left W.E. Forster.

In England Forster was almost totally to ignore the findings of the Newcastle Commission, which had taken three years to produce, using five commissioners and ten assistant commissioners. Forster instead relied on evidence from a small-scale study, which took a few months to complete, in four towns, by two inspectors, J.G. Fitch and D.R. Fearon in 1869. Discrepancies between the data presented to Forster and in the Newcastle Commission stem from the fact that the small-scale study takes as given the school age to be from 5–13 years, that is eight years of schooling. However, the Newcastle Commission interprets school age as 5–11 years, so only six years (or in fact, as it was, 5.7 years). The school leaving age was not raised to 12 years old until 1899 and therefore the Newcastle Commission is in fact accurate. The study used by Forster from Fitch and Fearon showed children to be missing from school when in fact they were not supposed to be in school above the age of 11 years anyway. Irrespective of the discrepancy, Forster's 1870 Bill was introduced. According to James Tooley it was meant:

> explicitly as a measure to cater for those children who were not being provided by existing voluntary measures. It was not designed to cater universally for all children, but only to fill in the gaps in the current private system … Forster was aware that voluntary private provision was a very valuable resource in educational provision, and simply needed to be supplemented by his new board schools as required, not replaced.[48]

So, just as in India, before the state intervened in education there was a vibrant schools' market operating in England and Wales, catering for the majority of school-aged children. State intervention initiated through the 1870 Act was only meant to fill in the gaps, not replace it. But, at the time, there were some critics of private schools, especially regarding quality, who would have been happy to see the system replaced. Just as with Hartog and Macaulay, what were their arguments to try to dismiss the private sector?

Quality

As in India, in England there were those who questioned the quality of the private schools, especially with respect to the teachers who typically had no teacher training. Even though parents at the time were happy to pay for their children to be taught by untrained teachers, some advising the government regarded teachers to have 'picked up' their knowledge 'promiscuously'.[49] According to Mr Cumin who was concerned about the mushrooming of private schools in the 1850s and as he set out his concerns in the Royal Commission on Popular Education of 1861:

> Of the private school masters in Devonport, one had been a blacksmith and afterwards an exciseman, another was a journeyman tanner, a third a clerk in a solicitor's office, a fourth (who was very successful in preparing lads for the competitive examination in the dockyards) keeps an evening school and works as a dockyard labourer, a fifth was a seaman, and others had been engaged in other callings.[50]

This, therefore, Mr Cumin believed was an illustration of the poor quality of teaching. However Mr Cumin need not have been concerned because parents were well aware that some teachers could try to hoodwink them by not being up to par. But as argued by West, parents were shrewd and could detect and reject such 'quacks'.[51]

The teacher training of the day shows an obsession with learning by rote. In the Royal Commission on Popular Education of 1861 a Mr Altick comments thus:

> the institutions that fed teachers into the expanding elementary school system were pedant factories, whose machinery efficiently removed whatever traces of interest in human culture the scholars had somehow picked up earlier in their careers.[52]

West makes the point that Mr Cumin's concerns may have been unfounded and agrees with Mr Altick that children were probably more inspired by the professionally eclectic teachers in the private schools who still retained their own personality and experience whilst teaching, as opposed to the trained teachers teaching by rote with their young wards repeating parrot fashion paragraphs to be memorised.

Even so, the lack of teacher training is not an argument for the introduction of the Board School through the 1870 Act. A rule could have been passed where private school teachers were required to undertake some training. But with regard to quality, it was the parents, paying fees, who were the inspectors of the private schools, being able to withdraw their children from a school they felt inefficient. Parents felt they needed to pay for schooling in order for it to be accountable to them and maintain efficiency. Evidence from the day shows that the majority of parents could pay and wanted to pay for schooling, according to the Newcastle Report:

> Almost all the evidence goes to show that though the offer of gratuitous education might be accepted by a certain proportion of the parents, it would in general be otherwise. The sentiment of independence is strong, and it is wounded by the offer of an absolutely gratuitous education.[53]

After 1870 – Unfair Competition

Between 1833 and 1870 schools could be funded in three ways: by subscriptions, fees or state subsidies. After 1870 an additional method was introduced, that of being funded by the local rate, which was a property tax. School boards were to look for gaps, either where private schools were not operating or where private provision was of low quality and hence 'inefficient', in order to set up a new Board School. Private schools now faced new unfair competition as Board Schools, funded through the rates, could drop their fees below those of the private schools. Parents were now also paying rates to support the Board Schools and had less disposable income, thus having to make new choices with regard to school spending. Private schools were being forced out of business, being crowded out by the cheaper public alternative. The letter quoted below is from a rector, whose schools (the St Paul's Church of England schools) were to be taken over by the new board as they were deemed to no longer be 'flourishing' and hence had declined in quality. They were no longer 'flourishing' because they were facing competition from a Board School in the same street, which was providing education at a lower cost to parents and giving students free books and slates. As in his letter of 1876 to the Manchester School Board the rector explains:

> Let it not be imagined that I am opposed to giving a cheap and good education to the people, if their circumstances require it, I would gladly aid to the utmost of my power in providing for the education of their children at the lowest possible charges. But I submit that their circumstances do not require it. They are well able to pay, as they have done heretofore, 6d and 8d per week ... I would ask whether it is right to pay out of the public rates for the education of children where parents are well able to pay for themselves? And is it right to members of Christian Churches, which have made great sacrifices of time and money to erect schools in connection with their places of worship, to set up rival schools which, as ratepayers, they are compelled to support, in addition to their having to support their own denominational schools?[54]

The unfair competition continued where funding could be increased to the Board Schools through public revenues. Section 54 of the Education Act 1870 allows for 'any sum required to meet any deficiency in the school fund, whether for satisfying past or future liabilities, shall be paid by the rating authority out of the local rate'.[55] The Board Schools drove out the private ones, propped up by taxation, irrespective of quality, patronised by parents who could no longer afford to pay private school fees in addition to the new taxes. What started out as a minor intervention in order to allow for universal education by filling in the gaps, gathered momentum.

Why?

West uses public choice theory to assert that those driving the idea of the new Board Schools were acting in self-interest, wishing to maximise the size, power and influence of the education bureau. According to West and public choice theory, those working in the bureau will want their budget to expand and if the budget of the bureau:

> can be expected to expand faster with the gradual establishment of a universal system of public schooling that benefits the children of middle income parents as well as the poorest, this system will be 'pushed' ... even if the poorest would do better in a smaller selective system wherein all the benefits went to them exclusively.[56]

The interests of the poor will be overtaken by the self-interest of those working in the education bureau. It was made explicit in 1870 through the Bill presented by W.E. Forster that it was of the utmost importance not to destroy the private schools' system that already existed. However, this was not to be the case as the private schools were crowded out, and according to West 'the actual events, it seems, were much more the consequence of discretionary bureau behaviour' than Parliament had wanted.[57]

SUMMING UP

What this chapter has shown is that in both nineteenth-century England and India an indigenous private school system existed without state intervention. In India in the 1820s and 1830s children were getting an education, some in 'school', others at home, the same in England. By the 1850s almost every child was in school. And in both cases, when the survey and census data were being collected the most important message conveyed was that care must be taken not to tamper with all that was good in the existing private system.

According to Munro, in India 'everything of this kind ought to be carefully avoided, and the people should be left to manage their schools in their own way'. And in England, Forster along with others reiterated that it was important not to destroy the private system but just to fill in any gaps if they existed. To re-quote Henry Brougham, 'it behoves us to take the greatest care how we interfere with a system which prospers so well of itself'.[58]

But it was not to be. In both India and England the whole government process steamrollered ahead and over what already existed, replacing it over the years with a virtually monopolistic government school system, funded, regulated and provided by the state. The message here is that all that was good was destroyed, crowded out, not able to compete. Even when those initially involved in a process to discover how children were being educated had indicated otherwise.

The following chapter investigates another kind of intervention by developed country governments, the giving of international aid. It asks: is bilateral and multilateral aid – known as systematic aid – making a positive difference to the lives of the poor? Its main focus is on India and schooling, but to begin the general debate regarding the why and how of aid giving is considered.

NOTES

1. Hartwell (1995), p. 42.
2. Tooley (2008), p. 123.
3. Dharampal (1995), p. 6.
4. Ibid.
5. Ibid.
6. Ibid.
7. Ibid., p. 90.
8. Ibid., p. 89.
9. Ibid.
10. Ibid.
11. Ibid., p. 90.
12. Ibid.
13. Ibid., pp. 18–19, pp. 34–5.
14. Adam (1841), p. 268, emphasis added; Leitner (1883), p. 349; cited in Dharampal (1995), p. 12.
15. Adam (1841), cited in Dharampal (1995), p. 6.
16. Ibid., p. 7.
17. Dharampal (1995), p. 18.
18. Ibid., p. 143; Cooke's data collected in 1823.
19. 1 anna = 1/16 of a rupee.
20. Dharampal (1995), p. 273.
21. Ibid., p. 233.
22. Ibid., p. 99.
23. Ibid., p. 129.
24. Ibid., p. 132.
25. Ibid., p. 160.

26. Ibid., p. 147.
27. Ibid.
28. Ibid., p. 270.
29. Ibid., p. 274.
30. Ibid., p. 279.
31. Ibid., p. 375.
32. Grey (2010).
33. Ibid., p. 90.
34. Young (1957), p. 729.
35. *The Economic Times of India*, Bombay edition, 31 January 1966.
36. Tooley and Stanfield (2003), p. 24.
37. West (1994), third edition of *Education and the State*, p. 158.
38. *The Report of the Poor Law Commissioners* (1841), cited in West (1994), p. 161.
39. *Minutes of the Committee of Council on Education* (1840–1841), cited in West (1994), p. 161.
40. Report on the State of Education in the Borough of Kingston upon Hull, *Journal of the Statistical Society of London*, July 1841, in West (1994), pp. 162–3.
41. West (1994), p. 165.
42. Ibid., pp. 170–1.
43. Brougham (1835), quoted in West (1994), p. 173.
44. Census 1851, pp. 134–5, cited in West (1994), p. 175.
45. Education Commission, *Report of the Commissioners Appointed to Enquire into The State of Popular Education in England*, Vol. I (1861), p. 85, cited in West (1994), p. 178.
46. West (1994), p. 179.
47. Education Commission, *Report of the Commissioners Appointed to Enquire into The State of Popular Education in England*, Vol. I (1861), p. 293, cited in West (1994), p. 213.
48. Tooley (2008), pp. 94–5.
49. West (1994), p. 208.
50. *The Royal Commission on Popular Education*, Vol. 1 (1861), p. 93, cited in West (1994), pp. 208–9.
51. West (1994), p. 208.
52. Newcastle Commission, p. 162, cited in West (1994), p. 210.
53. Newcastle Report, p. 73, cited in West (1994), p. 213.
54. West (1994), pp. 197–8.
55. Ibid., p. 193.
56. West (1975), p. 63.
57. Ibid., p. 72.
58. Brougham (1835), quoted in West (1994), p. 173.

2 Hostages to a fortune? – Schooling and international aid

INTRODUCTION TO DEVELOPMENT AID

The giving of aid is a relatively recent phenomenon. Stimulated by the success of the Marshall Plan in 1948, when the USA provided around $13 billion for the reconstruction of Europe after World War II, it was argued by economists such as John Maynard Keynes that similar outcomes could be achieved in developing countries. The Marshall Plan became 'the model for future foreign aid programmes'.[1] The USA kick-started economic recovery in Europe. It was claimed therefore that this demonstrated the possibility of developed countries stimulating growth in poor ones by providing them with aid.

Economic, moral and political validations are typically presented to justify the giving of aid. In economic terms providing poor countries with financial aid, the hypothesis goes, will stimulate investment, thus encouraging economic growth. Poverty traps can be broken by investments which generate greater productivity and growth; hence the eventual eradication of poverty.[2] Thus foreign aid will promote growth and development by filling a financing gap that exists in poor developing countries. Poverty traps cause illiteracy, poor health, low savings, population growth and poor infrastructure. The only way to break the cycle and the trap is for developed nations to provide investments into all of these areas. This relationship between providing foreign aid and stimulating economic growth and thus eradicating poverty traps was the view of the Pearson and Brandt Reports of the 1960s and 1980s.[3]

Political and moral reasons are also presented to justify the giving of international aid. The transfer of resources from rich to poor countries is regarded as a type of international welfare state, a humanitarian case favouring welfare as a means of a transferral of wealth based on Rawls' theory of justice.[4]

The political arguments as set out by some international aid agencies and academics, including Jeffrey Sachs, include ensuring national and international security and stability. Public statements from the Department for International Development in the UK (DfID) have claimed that aid to

India as well as Afghanistan and Pakistan has strategic benefits in terms of indirect national security benefits.[5] The US National Security Strategy, 2010, also makes the point that the US government is 'pursuing a range of specific initiatives in areas such as food security and global health that will be essential to the future security and prosperity of nations and peoples around the globe'[6] and that:

> Development is a strategic, economic, and moral imperative. We are focusing on assisting developing countries and their people to manage security threats, reap the benefits of global economic expansion, and set in place accountable and democratic institutions that serve basic human needs.[7]

However, it is not just the provision of aid that makes a difference. Focus needs to be on *effective* aid. Having a positive effect on economic growth and aiding the poorest is crucial; just giving money is not enough.

This chapter talks about systematic aid – bilateral and multilateral – not emergency aid. Systematic aid generally consists of the transferral of cash in the form of concessional loans or grants. Concessional loans are typically provided at below market interest rates over long periods of time. Grants may be given by a developed nation without expecting anything back, and according to Moyo 'grants are viewed as free resources and could therefore perfectly substitute for a government's domestic revenues'.[8]

In September 2000 the Millennium Development Summit was held at the United Nations (UN) in New York. It brought together world leaders who agreed to the adoption of the UN Millennium Declaration aimed at reducing extreme poverty by 2015. The UN Millennium Declaration made a commitment to free 'the entire human race from extreme poverty'. Emerging from the declaration were the eight Millennium Development Goals (MDGs). These focus on reducing poverty and hunger, empowering women and stimulating gender equality, improving health and access to education, as well as ensuring environmental sustainability. These objectives were designed to halve poverty by 2015 using 1990 as a baseline.

Eradicating poverty is the concern of the whole international community and measuring its progress is of the utmost importance as stated by the Secretary General of the UN, Ban Ki-moon:

> Eradicating extreme poverty continues to be one of the main challenges of our time, and is a major concern of the international community. Ending this scourge will require the combined efforts of all, governments, civil society organizations and the private sector, in the context of a stronger and more effective global partnership for development. The Millennium Development Goals set time bound targets, by which progress in reducing income poverty, hunger, disease, lack of adequate shelter and exclusion – while promoting gender

equality, health, education and environmental sustainability – can be measured. They also embody basic human rights – the rights of each person on the planet to health, education, shelter and security. The Goals are ambitious but feasible and, together with the comprehensive United Nations development agenda, set the course for the world's efforts to alleviate extreme poverty by 2015.[9]

However, according to The Millennium Development Goals Report 2011, although advances have been made in certain areas progress has been uneven, with disparities between and within countries. What seems more daunting is the admission that the hardest to reach, the most vulnerable, are still benefitting the least from international aid.[10] In addition, there have been some doubts raised as to whether the actual goals themselves and the methods of evaluating progress are the most appropriate ones for reducing poverty.

Some believe that one more big push could inject the crucial spurt required for the MDGs to successfully stride towards the 2015 finishing line. In order to do so, economists such as Jeffrey Sachs, Director of The Earth Institute at Colombia University and Special Adviser to the UN Secretary-General Ban Ki-moon on the MDGs, are calling for developed nations to commit more money for development assistance. Sachs and the UN deem that rich countries should contribute 0.7 per cent of their Gross National Income (GNI) to Official Development Assistance (ODA). Hence, the best way to end extreme poverty in developing countries is for rich ones to provide them with more financial aid.[11] More aid will increase the likelihood that some of the MDGs will be met by 2015. In Sachs' book *The End of Poverty* he maintains that by 2025 extreme poverty around the world can end and that the MDGs can be met by 2015 if rich countries provide the financial help they promised. Getting the poorest nations' feet on the development ladder will allow 'the tremendous dynamism of self sustaining economic growth' to take hold. But this will only happen with the 'big push'. According to Sachs:

> nothing short of a massive co-ordinated development effort, a big push, is needed if sustained poverty reduction and the achievement of the Millennium Development Goals is to be realised within an acceptable time horizon.[12]

Note the 'massive co-ordinated development effort'.

However, with regard to education and schooling the MDGs' focus on enrolment could have been a mistake, as Jishnu Das and his colleagues put it:

> the Millennium Development Goals call for universal primary education and equal enrollments among girls and boys, but say nothing about learning and

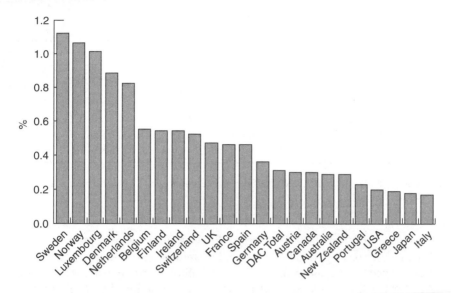

Source: http://www.dfid.gov.uk/Documents/publications1/sid2010/SID-2010.pdf.

Figure 2.1 *Comparison of provisional net ODA/GNI ratios for DAC donors 2009*

competency. Similarly, a number of educational interventions focus on getting children into schools (midday meals, free textbooks, stipends for girls are all examples from very recent history) but do not monitor what these children learn and what effect these interventions have on their learning. This may be a mistake. Although all children in Pakistan may be enrolled in primary schools by 2015, many may complete their education functionally illiterate and innumerate.[13]

Currently five countries give 0.7 per cent of GNI for ODA; these are primarily Scandinavian ones, including Sweden, Norway and the Netherlands. The USA is the largest donor of international aid in monetary terms at just over £18 billion[14] ($28.26 billion) per year, accounting for around 0.21 per cent of GNI. Germany gives 0.38 per cent. Figure 2.1 sets out comparisons of ODA/GNI ratios for the DAC (Development Assistance Committee) donors.

As Table 2.1 shows, UK ODA for 2011 reached around 0.56 per cent of UK GNI, estimated to be around £8,570 million ($13,455 million), of which £5,004 million ($7,856 million) was bilateral ODA and £3,566 million ($5,598 million) multilateral ODA. UK bilateral ODA to Asia accounts for £1,289 million ($2,024 million) compared to £1,961 million ($3,079 million)

Table 2.1   ODA UK bilateral aid by region (£ million)

Region	Aid
Asia	£1,289 million ($2,024 m)
Africa	£1,961 million ($3,079 m)
Rest of the world	£66 million ($104 m)
Non-specific regions	£1,688 million ($2,650 m)
Total UK ODA 2011	£8,570 million (bilateral: £5,004 million ($7,856 m); multilateral: £3,566 million ($5,598m))

Source: OECD, http://stats.oecd.org/Index.aspx?datasetcode=TABLE1 ($ may not add owing to rounding).

to Africa, of which £1,942 million ($3,079 million) goes to sub-Saharan Africa. The 'rest of the world' totals £66 million ($104 million) and 'non region specific' £1,688 million ($2,650 million). An increase to 0.7 per cent for the UK would amount to around £11.4 billion ($17.9 billion) (an increase then of £3 billion ($4.71 billion)) being spent on international aid.[15]

Most economists would agree that in order to eliminate extreme poverty then the necessary condition for doing so is sustained growth.[16] But does providing aid to poor countries lead to sustained growth?

AID SCEPTICS

Not everyone agrees with Sachs and the UN that aid is necessary for economic growth. Indeed some point out that providing international aid to developing countries, which in some cases do not have well-functioning institutions or the rule of law, is very different from post-war Europe receiving aid through the Marshall Plan. Therefore, basing international aid to developing countries on the successful rebuilding of Europe is very controversial. According to Brian Snowdon:

> Inefficient institutions, created and perpetuated by elites are a major barrier to progress in many developing countries ... we should not be surprised when aid flowing into an environment dominated by mismanaged or corrupt institutions and inadequate governance fails to deliver a virtuous circle of enlightened reforms and the Holy Grail of sustained economic growth.[17]

Aid critics, such as Dambisa Moyo, argue that aid just does not work. In fact 'the more it infiltrates, the more it erodes, the greater the culture of aid-dependency'.[18] Moyo posits that 'aid has helped make the poor poorer and growth slower'.[19] Rather than promoting growth and development, 'systematic' aid leads to the expansion of government bureaucracies into which the aid flows.[20] Aid, she argues, benefits the political elite, propping up 'corrupt governments – providing them with freely usable cash'[21] that is typically mismanaged, stolen and disappears through bribery, fraudulent claims and outright theft. It is the inefficient institutions created by the elites in developing countries that are the major barriers to progress.[22]

The ultimate aim is sustainable development, not a dependency culture,[23] yet typically, according to Moyo:

> Aid has not lived up to expectations. It remains at the heart of the development agenda, despite the fact that there are very compelling reasons to show that it perpetuates the cycle of poverty and derails sustainable economic growth.[24]

But still the giving of aid continues. Why? Moyo and others believe it is because systematic aid is big business, a well-oiled industry upon which many are dependent, including the aid agencies themselves. Not only do the aid agencies benefit but so do the donors motivated by 'self interested political foreign policy considerations'.[25] Joseph Hanlon et al. agree:

> Aid has not failed: what has failed is an aid and anti-poverty industry that thrives on complexity and mystification, with highly paid consultants designing ever more complicated projects for 'the poor' and continuing to impose policy conditions on poor countries.[26]

And Hollis Chenery in 1964 admitted that:

> the main objective of foreign assistance, as of many other tools of foreign policy, is to produce the kind of political and economic environment in the world in which the United States can best pursue its own social goals.[27]

The allocation of aid, agrees Roger Riddell, is 'shaped by the political, commercial and strategic interests of donors'.[28] These influences on aid reduce the impact it can have for the poor, by at least one-third or even more.[29]

Moyo's thesis conforms to the earlier views of aid sceptics such as Milton Friedman and Lord Peter Bauer. They also argued that international aid could in fact reduce rather than increase economic growth.[30] The reduction in growth could occur owing to the effect the financial inflow would have on the developing country's government bureaucracies both in respect of their power and quality. International aid could encourage:

wasteful investment projects, corruption, the suppression of local entrepreneurial talent, the undermining of incentives, and the enrichment of entrenched
elite groups who have little interest in economic progress.[31]

Paul Collier agrees:

> aid alone is really unlikely ... to be able to address the problems of the bottom
> billion, and it has become so highly politicized that its design is often pretty
> dysfunctional.[32]

He suggests that aid should be focused on the 'traps' that make and perpetuate a country's poverty; for example, being in conflict, being landlocked
with 'bad' neighbours, enjoying rich natural resources and experiencing
poor governance. However, Collier also thinks that 'the key obstacle to
reforming aid is public opinion'.[33] Although he regards the MDGs to have
been a step forward he also criticises them for being too widely focused
so that the bottom billion 'get lost in the general babble'.[34] Collier does
suggest channelling more aid through independent service authorities such
as private firms, non-governmental organisations (NGOs) and churches,
thus shifting services, such as health and education, away from the public
sector creating employment opportunities in the private one, thus stimulating providers who deliver.

William Easterly and George Ayittey are also recent critics of the
effectiveness of international aid.[35] Easterly sees the main problems to be
associated with 'Planners' taking control of the allocation of aid rather
than 'Searchers':

> A Planner thinks he already knows the answers; he thinks of poverty as a
> technical engineering problem that his answers will solve. A Searcher admits he
> doesn't know the answers in advance; he believes that poverty is a complicated
> tangle of political, social, historical, institutional and technological factors. A
> Searcher hopes to find answers to individual problems only by trial and error
> experimentation. A Planner believes outsiders know enough to impose solu-
> tions. A Searcher believes only insiders have enough knowledge to find solu-
> tions, and that most solutions must be home grown.[36]

Without local knowledge it is highly unlikely that Planners are able to
target transfers to the most needy in the required quantities or for the most
appropriate and effective projects. Aid needs to get to the poorest in the
most effective way to make the most difference to their lives.

Chicago economists, including Harry Johnson and Milton Friedman,
agreeing with the Searchers principle, propose that it is the market mechanism that can stimulate growth and efficiency in developing economies,
not government planning. Friedman had a special concern for developing

countries, emphasising the importance of encouraging the emergence of entrepreneurial personalities. Friedman argues that:

> [w]hat is required in underdeveloped countries is the release of the energies of millions of able, active, and vigorous people ... an atmosphere of freedom, of maximum opportunity for people to experiment, and of incentive for them to do so in an environment in which there are objective tests of success and failure – in short a vigorous, free capitalistic market.[37]

Friedman highlights a major problem, as does Easterly, with international aid allocated by Planners. There is a crucial difference between spending one's own money and money acquired from external sources. With your own money 'you clearly have a strong incentive both to economise and to get as much value as you can for each dollar you spend'.[38] Spending someone else's money on someone else is very different. There is much less care and concern about how much and where someone else's money is spent. According to Friedman, when someone is put in a position of deciding what is good for others 'the effect is to instil in the one group a feeling of almost God-like power; in the other, a feeling of childlike dependence'.[39] The result? Typically a waste of scarce resources and a failure to achieve the intended objectives.

The damaging unintended consequences of systematic aid can include negative effects on local entrepreneurs. Consider an example where aid is used to supply a good for 'free', in this case schooling materials such as free textbooks that originally or typically would be produced locally, which owing to international aid Planners are now given to the community free of cost. Local entrepreneurs can no longer compete with 'free' materials and hence go out of business. These businesses used to employ staff. The former staff now cannot take care of their families as they have lost their incomes. Local textbook production is stifled owing to the giving away of free imports provided by, say, the British government international aid programme. In years to come when international aid no longer supports the giving of free textbooks, and the textbooks need replacing, there are now no local producers as they were previously put out of business by international aid.

But does anyone consider these unintended consequences?

Friedrich Hayek, in his seminal paper *The Use of Knowledge in Society*, deliberates how Planners could not amass the information required to effectively allocate resources. It is only through the price mechanism and through individual actions and knowledge that problems can be solved. For Hayek:

> those who clamour for 'conscious direction' ... cannot believe that anything which has evolved without design (and even without our understanding it) should solve problems which we should not be able to solve consciously.[40]

Aid agencies have been accused of having a 'resistance to knowledge' and 'lazy thinking'. Aid agencies' recommendations have, according to some, shown a 'lack of distinction made between strategies founded on the hard evidence provided by randomised trials or natural experiments'.[41]

Yet Easterly does believe that aid could make differences if the bureaucratic problems through which systematic aid needs to flow could be corrected, or indeed bypassed. Targeting aid through Searchers at the grass-roots level could provide a much better framework for distributing and allocating aid that would be effectively utilised.

Similarly, Ayittey deems there to be two types of elite in developing countries: the Hippos and the Cheetahs. The Hippos are from the 1950s and 1960s generation; the Cheetahs are the young graduates, entrepreneurs with dynamism wanting change who are no longer happy to watch the mismanagement of resources and aid. The Hippo generation is described by Ayittey as:

> stodgy, pudgy, and wedded to the old colonialism/imperialism paradigm with an abiding faith in the potency of the state. They sit tight in their air-conditioned government offices, comfortable in their belief that the state can solve all problems. All the state needs is more power. And they ferociously defend their territory since that is what provides them with their wealth. The whole country may collapse around them, but they are content as long as their pond is secure.[42]

Hippos are a big part of the aid problem, not just through the misallocation of funds, but also owing to bribery, corruption and waste. However, Sachs suggests that 'the focus on corruption and governance is exaggerated'.[43]

But according to Ayittey:

> A bucket full of holes can only hold a certain amount of water for a certain amount of time. Pouring in more water makes little sense, as it will all drain away. To the extent that there are internal leaks in Africa – corruption, senseless civil wars, wasteful military expenditure, capital flight, and government waste – pouring in more foreign aid makes little sense.[44]

So why not leave it up to the Searchers and the Cheetahs? Could great strides to the finishing line not be made by changing to bottom-up approaches? Indeed, that is the argument put by C.K. Prahalad in his book *The Fortune At the Bottom of the Pyramid*:

> If we stop thinking of the poor as victims or as a burden and start recognizing them as resilient and creative entrepreneurs and value conscious consumers, a whole new world of opportunity will open up.[45]

Agreed. So what of aid to India? The following part of the chapter goes on to consider aid to India. Generally, what does aid to India look like? How much is it? And where does the money given to improve education go?

AID TO INDIA

In 2009–2010 India was the top recipient of UK bilateral aid, receiving £295 million ($463 million), with Ethiopia a close second (£214 million ($336 million)) and Bangladesh some way behind in third position (£149 million ($234 million)). In 2012, the British government, represented by the Secretary of State Andrew Mitchell, announced that the UK is 'walking the last mile' with regard to aid to India.[46] However, there are still many poor people living in India, irrespective of the success it has seen in terms of economic growth over the last few decades. For the period 2011–2012 India enjoyed growth at around 6.5 per cent.[47]

According to the 2011 UNDP Human Development Report, 41.6 per cent of India's population are living on less than $1.25 PPP per day.[48] The Multidimensional Poverty Index (MPI) indicates there are some 421 million poor people living in eight of the most deprived Indian states, which include Bihar, Uttar Pradesh and West Bengal.[49]

DfID are to spend £280 ($440) million per year in India until 2015,[50] with the main focus being on assisting the poorest in three low-income states, namely Madhya Pradesh, Bihar and Orissa (although five other states – Chhattisgarh, Jharkhand, Rajasthan, Uttar Pradesh and West Bengal will also receive support with certain programmes). Women and girls have been put at the heart of the DfID agenda. Aid money is going to be used to invest in girls' education as well as to focus on safe births, children's healthcare, nutrition and sanitation.

The World Bank in 2012 funded around 80 projects in India. Support included $9.2 billion of loans from the International Development Association (IDA), which were interest free credits used for active World Bank projects aimed at the poor; $14.6 billion from the International Bank for Reconstruction and Development (IBRD) and $3.57 billion from the International Finance Corporation (IFC).

AID TO SCHOOLING IN INDIA: A BRIEF HISTORY

The 1990 World Conference on Education for All at Jomtien, Thailand, proposed the attainment of universal primary education by 2000. After the conference the World Bank, DfID and the United Nations Children's

Fund (UNICEF) announced their intentions to increase their support and focus on primary schooling. India was to become one of the recipients of aid as according to the official figures in the late 1980s some 30–40 million primary-aged children were out of school in India. According to Christopher Colclough, India was going to need more than one million new primary school places every year if the situation with regard to children's enrolment in primary school was not going to get any worse.[51] In India during the 1990s there was a shift of aid allocation towards the social sector (including education) reaching a peak of about one quarter of total aid to India in 2000. Aid that contributed to expenditure on India's elementary education (Classes 1–8) rose from 10 per cent in 1993–1994 to 35 per cent in 2000–2001. International aid was used for the first time to improve the quality and quantity of primary schooling in 1986. One of the first projects to be funded by British overseas development assistance was the Andhra Pradesh Primary Education Project (APPEP), which focused on training teachers and improving the quality of buildings and classrooms. This was followed by various other initiatives such as the Shiksha Karmi Project (1987), which focused on improving teacher quality and reducing absenteeism, and the Mahila Samakhya Project (1988–1990), focusing on empowering women from disadvantaged backgrounds funded by the Swedish and Dutch respectively. In 1993–1994, aid to education increased substantially and saw for the first time multiple funders contributing in conjunction with the Government of India (GOI) to fund the District Primary Education Programme (DPEP). This involved contributions from the World Bank, EU, DfID, UNICEF and the Netherlands. The aim of this project was to provide quality education for 6–14 year olds in chosen districts and states. In 2001–2002 the GOI launched the Sarva Shiksha Abhiyan (SSA) programme that was to 'absorb' all existing externally aided programmes, including DPEP. Some aid donors pulled out of India in 1998 owing to their nuclear testing programme and others were forced out and decided to no longer provide aid to India in 2003 when the newly elected Bharatiya Janata Party (BJP) changed government policy on aid. Only six bilateral donors along with multilateral agencies were to provide aid to India. It was possible for those who were now excluded to support directly NGOs. However, in 2004 the Congress Party were installed and once more all bilateral aid was welcomed. However, some bilateral donors decided to either exit or reduce aid to India:

> The bilateral aid programmes of Canada, Denmark, Italy, France, Norway, Netherlands and Sweden were either not renewed or were reduced to insignificant proportions after 2003, as were grants from UNICEF, IFAD and Ford.[52]

One of the most significant donors to pull out with regard to schooling were the Swedes who through the Swedish International Development Cooperation Agency (SIDA) had been funding two programmes in Rajasthan – Shiksha Kami and Lok Jumbish.

After 2003 (within what is called the Tenth Plan period) the only donors to India's elementary education were the World Bank, DfID and the European Commission (EC). When the GOI launched SSA it found itself with insufficient funds in the Tenth Plan period to finance the programme. It therefore approached its only remaining bilateral partners, the World Bank (IDA), DfID and the EC, for support. The total projected cost of SSA was estimated at $3.5 billion. The donors contributed around one-third of this ($1.046 billion) with 48 per cent of that coming from the World Bank, 33 per cent from DfID, and 19 per cent from the EC. GOI funded 45 per cent ($1.58 billion) and Indian states the remaining 25 per cent ($875 million). However, expenditure on SSA from 2003–2004 to 2006–2007 ran to $7.8 billion, with the fixed monetary contributions from the donors as stated above. In 2007 a further $1 billion of external aid for SSA was agreed. Some believe that this spending had positive effects although:

> aid to education in India did not serve to change the priorities of the Indian government it did act to strengthen them ... the substantial unmet needs of the poorest families in India, very many of whose children had had no access to schooling prior to DPEP/SSA, were certainly served better by the application of India's priorities to universalise primary/elementary schooling during the past two decades ... the agencies can reasonably claim credit in having encouraged, and helped to strengthen that process.[53]

DEVELOPMENT AND SCHOOLING

With regard to education, Goal 2 of the MDGs sets out the aim of achieving universal primary education. That is, to 'ensure, that by 2015, children everywhere, boys and girls alike, will be able to complete a full course of primary schooling'.[54] Indeed, Goal 3 also states with regard to gender equality and the empowerment of women that there needs to be the elimination of 'gender disparity in primary and secondary education, preferably by 2005, and to all levels of education no later than 2015'.[55] In order to ascertain whether these goals have been met the indicators that determine success, or not, include measuring the:

- net enrolment ratio in primary education;
- proportion of pupils starting grade 1 who reach the last grade of primary;
- literacy rate of 15–24 year olds, women and men.[56]

According to the UN, in 2011 Goal 2 had some way to go before being met. Around 87 per cent of children in the developing world are estimated to complete primary education and in about half of the 'least developed countries' only three out of every five children in primary school carry on until the last grade.[57] However, a warning with respect to official figures must be highlighted here. In most countries the existence of low-cost private unrecognised/unregistered schools has not been taken into account in these figures and those children gaining an education within them have typically been 'assumed' to be 'out of school' or included in the out of school figures.[58] Low-cost unrecognised/unregistered schools often exist and operate under the radar of official statistics. It has only been in the past couple of years that their existence has begun to be acknowledged. Only census data carried out through household surveys would pick up on children's attendance at low-cost private unrecognised schools.

Before proceeding it must be said that completing a full course of primary schooling in India as targeted by the MDGs may be a goal that in fact has little meaning. Why? This will be explored in more detail through the rest of this chapter and the following one, but attending government schools, especially in poor parts of India and other developing countries, can actually have very little impact on children's achievement or learning. Teacher absenteeism and lethargy combined with poor quality facilities add little to a child's attainment. It seems rational for children to drop out early from such a system because the poor quality implies an almost non-existent educational value.[59]

Why is it that 'experts' such as Jeffrey Sachs and others do not seem to appreciate that children who do not complete primary education may not do, in some circumstances, partly owing to choice? Choice, because their parents being rational and acting in their own self-interest will have recognised that their children are attending a school where teachers typically are absent or do not teach. Learning very little or nothing at all would make any parent withdraw their children from education that costs money in terms of uniform, books, transport and time. If teachers are not turning up to teach and learning is almost non-existent then not completing primary schooling is rational.[60]

Indeed, the MDG goal concerning the completion of primary education seems to have missed out on a very important word – 'quality'. Only when schooling has any quality will it actually provide value to those studying. Completing primary education of quality means something, completing primary education without quality is no goal at all.

AID TO SCHOOLING IN INDIA

With regard to schooling, DfID are planning, over the next four years, to build secondary schools, train teachers and cover the costs of girls attending school. The attention is to be on dalit and tribal girls. The aim is to 'support over 800,000 children to enrol in secondary school and 1.5 million children to enrol in primary school'.[61] DfID are to spend £280 ($440) million per year in India until 2015.[62] The total amount going to education out of the £280 ($440) million budget per year is as shown in Table 2.2. Around 19 per cent (almost one-fifth) of the budget will be spent on education. The programmes include cash incentives for school attendance as well as the provision of bicycles for girls who attend secondary school. According to DfID their objective is to change children's lives through learning. Their focus is to train teachers, improve the quality of learning and to support children to attend secondary schooling, with an emphasis on girls:

> we will help girls stay in school beyond primary level to ensure they get the full benefit from education which will transform their lives and opportunities.[63]

The USA is supporting the Rashtriya Madhyamik Shiksha Abhiyan (RMSA) framework, which is focusing on the access to and improvement of the quality of secondary education/schools. The World Bank is contributing $500 million and the GoI and DfID are providing $12,306 million and $90 million respectively between 2012 and 2017 (a total of $12,896 million for the project). The money is going to be used, according to the World Bank, to expand 'promising pilot programs'. The project includes:

> Quality improvement activities include teacher professional development, recruitment of additional teachers, and capacity building of local institutions to support change. Access will be expanded through new and upgraded schools, especially in underserved areas, outreach to communities, more relevant learning materials and better teachers.[64]

Children between 15 and 16 years old are being targeted with having, by 2015, universal access to secondary education, with secondary schools being available within five kilometres of all households. Universal retention is also the focus by 2020. RMSA is looking to upgrade around 44,000 government upper primary schools to secondary schools through a construction programme and appointing the necessary teaching staff. The same goes for around 60,000 existing government secondary schools, which are also to be improved, expanded, repaired and renovated. A building programme of around 11,000 new secondary and senior secondary schools is proposed with a specific aim of provision in low-income

Table 2.2 DfID contributions to Indian education 2011–2015 (£ and $ million)

2011–2012		2012–2013		2013–2014		2014–2015		Total	
resource	capital	resource	capital	resource	capital	resource	capital	resource	capital
£53.6	£13.4	£60.6	£14.4	£27	£6	£29.8	£7.2	**£173.2**	**£40.8**
($84)	($21)	($95)	($22.6)	($42.4)	($9.4)	($46.8)	($11.3)	**($271.9)**	**($64.1)**
million	million	million	million	million	million	million	million	**million**	**million**
Proportion of total UK India aid 24%		Proportion of total UK India aid 26.8%		Proportion of total UK India aid 11.8%		Proportion of total UK India aid 13.2%		Proportion of total UK India aid 19%	

Source: DfID India Operational Plan 2011–2015, http://www.dfid.gov.uk/documents/publications1/op/india-2011.pdf.

areas. The programme aims to encourage those from weaker sections to attain and remain in secondary school. Quality improvements are being proposed by carrying out training, improving the curriculum and the utilisation of new materials and methods. According to the World Bank, 35 million students will 'benefit' annually by 2015.[65]

However, what could be described as a contradiction to the above plan seems to have been given in a speech by Caroline Anstey, Managing Director of the World Bank, in June 2012, where she argued that:

> Development is no longer about development experts in foreign capitals making suppositions about people in distant communities. Civil society matters for development effectiveness. A robust civil society can check on budgets, seek and publish information, challenge stifling bureaucracies, throw a spotlight on corruption, and monitor service delivery.[66]

Anstey also calls for:

> greater transparency, greater accountability and a much sharper focus on monitoring, evaluation and results – for taxpayers who need to see that the development funds they contribute are used effectively, especially in tough fiscal times; for citizens who need to know that their governments are using their money accountably; for evaluating interventions that can move countries towards growth and opportunity and away from aid dependence.[67]

So the funding of government-provided schooling is one of the main destinations of World Bank resources for schooling in India. But why? Anstey's speech calls for 'greater transparency, greater accountability' as well as the need for the effective use of aid money as verified by research findings through monitoring and evaluation of programmes. International aid money given to government schools has typically received a bad press. Research suggests that money ploughed into public schooling, in India as well as other developing countries, is actually making very little, if any, difference to student achievement.

The outcome of previous international aid funding to government schooling in India will be considered later, but it is important to ask: Why have international aid agencies not concluded that allocating more resources to government schooling may not be having the desired effect? The main issue is teachers' absenteeism and lack of activity, which aid is not targeting directly. There will not be an increase in student achievement outcomes within a government schools' system that does not provide what the majority of poor parents want, that is, English-medium schools and teachers who teach.

The main issue here is an ideological objection to the private schools' sector, perpetuated since governments jumped onto the saddle of the galloping horse not only in the UK and the US, but also in those countries ruled at the time through the Empire. This view seems to have gained pace and momentum, where now the general majority view would be an imperialistic one, namely that no developed nation has experienced a flourishing low-cost private schooling system, so how can this be part of the answer for developing nations?

The majority view in academia and politics seems to be, above everything else, that what has to be fixed is the currently incompetent state system, irrespective of the possibility of successful liberation, through people power, for millions of children and families from state schooling to low-cost private schools. Why?

So Only the State Will Do

Development experts like Jeffery Sachs believe that education needs to be provided by the governments of developing countries:

> Collective action, through effective government provision of health, education, infrastructure, as well as foreign assistance when needed, underpins economic success.[68]

Successful countries realised that there needed to be an active governmental role in education and hence schooling to 'ensure that every citizen has the chance and means (through public education, public health and basic infrastructure) to participate productively within the society'.[69]

But Sachs also supposes that:

> Experience has shown that private entrepreneurs do a much better job of running businesses than governments. When governments run businesses, they tend to do so for political rather than economic reasons. State enterprises tend to overstaff their operations, since jobs equal votes for politicians and layoffs can cost a politician the next election.[70]

So why does Sachs not see this in the case of education?

> Governments rarely have the in-house expertise to manage complex technologies, and they shouldn't, aside from sectors where the government's role is central, such as in defence, infrastructure, health and education.[71]

But, seemingly in contradiction, Sachs agrees that:

> to at least a small extent, households themselves can pay out of household income for some of their basic needs, for example, through purchases from private-sector providers.[72]

Indeed, quite positively he states that one goal for the years to come is to have:

A new approach to global problem solving based on cooperation among nations and the dynamism and creativity of the nongovernmental sector.[73]

But still, even though it has been shown that many poor parents are currently paying for low-cost private schooling in some parts of India, Sachs, the World Bank, to some extent the DfID and aid agencies such as UNESCO and Oxfam believe that the only thing to do is 'fix' government education systems.

According to UNESCO, low-cost private schools are not the answer because:

Transferring responsibility to communities, parents and private providers is not a substitute for fixing public sector education systems.

And

For the poorest groups, public investment and provision constitute the only viable route to an education that meets basic quality standards.[74]

The haphazardness of the market and the 'clearly unplanned' growth of the private schools' sector provide concerns for UNESCO. The 'overwhelming priority should be to improve their [government school] standards and accessibility rather than to channel public finance into the private sector'.[75] What follows is a warning. If state education systems are not fixed then there is a risk of 'creeping commercialisation' from low-fee private schools, and this will inevitably lead to 'rising inequality and the fragmentation of services and standards'.[76]

Markets, UNESCO believes, have their limits when it comes to schooling and it is vital to:

recognize the limits to choice and competition. The development of quasi-markets in education and the rapid emergence of low-fee private providers are *not* resolving underlying problems in access, equity or quality. While many actors have a role to play in education provision, there is *no* substitute for a properly financed and effectively managed state education system, especially at primary level.[77]

According to the critics, low-cost private schools can never cater for the poorest and therefore will not significantly contribute to achieving Education for All targets and the MDGs.[78] So even though the low-cost private schools' market is regarded as providing a 'short term solution to the educational needs of children in India today, it is unlikely to be the best means of providing education for all children in the longer term in ways that respect equity principles'.[79]

In summary:

> it is important to emphasise that in so far as it is unable to offer potential benefits to all children, and especially those children who may remain outside of formal schooling or drop-out early, there is little evidence that current growth in the private school sector will make a major positive contribution to the achievement of EFA goals.[80]

Those who propose that the fixing of the government schools' systems is the only way forward believe that the poorest are being marginalised by the private sector; that government schools are being 'ghettoized' by the disadvantaged and poorest groups in society, hence reinforcing inequalities.[81]

Indeed, Shiva Kumar et al. believe that private schools can just be regarded as another 'quick fix'; having created an impression of being a solution to India's schooling crisis, they actually are not.[82]

The second PROBE (Public Report on Basic Education in India) report says that private schools:

> are not very different from government schools. Their success in attracting children often hinges more on deception (for example, misleading claims of being 'English medium' or even 'convent' schools) than on actual quality.[83]

It is also argued, as in other reports and literature, that 'a privatised schooling system is fundamentally inequitable as schooling opportunities depend on one's ability to pay'. And that:

> [B]y perpetuating existing social inequalities, private schooling defeats one of the main purposes of 'universal elementary education' – breaking the old barriers of class, caste and gender in Indian society.[84]

Finally, the updated PROBE report irrespective of research findings believes that quick fixes, including private schools, 'have capsized on the rock of social inequality',[85] fixing government schools can be the only way forward. The report concludes that 'where there's a will there's a way'.

But whose will?

Surely, if UNESCO and others are regarding government schools to be attended only by the most disadvantaged, then one option would not be to fix the government system for the minority but to provide the minority with the opportunities being sought and enjoyed by others. In this regard targeted vouchers could be one way to allow all children choice. Cash transfers, either conditional or unconditional, could also allow the marginalised opportunities for choice. Such initiatives will be provided greater scrutiny and examination in Chapter 4. Those wanting and championing the idea of fixing a whole state system, which has had large amounts of money thrown at it already, is still in a state of disrepair and has become 'ghettoized' by the few, seems rather odd. Counterintuitive? Are we missing something? Not according to Kevin Watkins, who believes that:

> Some donors have responded to the crisis in education by advocating what they like to describe as 'innovative' solutions. One of them, favoured by the British government, is the use of aid to expand choice and competition in education through vouchers and support for low-fee private providers. While popular with libertarian and right-wing thinktanks, this is an idea that combines an implausible and ideologically driven faith in markets with a failure to confront the real challenge – namely, building public education systems that offer decent quality, free education to all children.[86]

Maybe we should point him in the direction of Hayek, where he states that:

> The value of freedom consists mainly in the opportunity for the growth of the un-designed, and the beneficial functioning of a free society rests largely on the existence of such freely grown institutions.[87]

But it is highly unlikely that those opposing parental choice so vehemently would even give such ideas the time of day.

CAN GOVERNMENT EDUCATION IN INDIA BE FIXED?

Trying to fix education through government initiatives as well as international aid has been going on for years. In India there have been many government schemes, which have targeted enrolment, quality and retention in schools. Since 1986 there has been an emphasis on elementary education in India through the National Policy on Education (NPE) and the Programme of Action (POA – in 1992). State-specific schemes have been followed by multi-state programmes such as Operation Blackboard (OB), the District Primary Education Programme (DPEP), Sarva Shiksha Abhiyan (SSA) and the National Programme of Nutritional Support to Primary Education (Midday Meal Scheme), each in their own way aiming at improving facilities, materials, access, achievement and retention in government primary schools.

Figures show that the whole of the education budget accounts for about 10.7 per cent of the Indian government's spending, which is around 3.1 per cent of gross domestic product (GDP). The proportion provided to elementary education is around 36 per cent,[88] accounting for 2 per cent or less of GDP. Since 2009 the budget for elementary education in India has doubled, increasing from Rs. 26,169 crore[89] (US$4,685.59 million[90]) in 2009–2010 to Rs. 55,746 crore (US$9,981.38 million) in 2011–2012. These figures include both central and state funding. Per child allocation has risen during the same time frame from Rs. 2,004 (US$35.88 per year) to Rs. 4,269 (US$76.43 per year). On average, 77 per cent of the education budget is invested in teacher and management costs, 15 per cent is spent on school infrastructure, with only around 7 per cent spent on interventions aimed directly at children, such as free text books, uniforms, etc.[91]

However, the state system in India is no further forward to being fixed now than it ever was because of the lack of classroom activity and teacher attendance.[92] A repeat in 2006 of the PROBE survey, initially carried out in 1996, shows that although enrolment and school infrastructure have improved, classroom activity has not.

The 'success' of increased enrolment needs to be viewed with care. It is very typical in government schools for children to be enrolled when indeed they do not 'attend'. Being marked as attending also does not mean the child is actually present on that day. Actual attendance has been shown to be much lower than registers denote: 'some children are only nominally enrolled; others are enrolled in both government and private schools; and still others attend only irregularly'.[93] Indeed during the updated PROBE survey 'the proportion of students present in school based on the register was 63 per cent of those enrolled'.[94] That is, almost 40 per cent of the enrolled children are not attending government schools in rural areas visited. So why is it that children do not attend 'free' government schools? The two main reasons are teacher absenteeism and teacher inactivity.

GOVERNMENT TEACHER ABSENTEEISM AND INACTIVITY

Research by the World Bank found teacher absenteeism in India's government schools to range between 15 and 42 per cent. Unannounced visits to 3700 government schools in 20 states produced some 35,000 observations on teacher attendance and activity. Where teachers were present, only half of them were teaching;[95] research has shown that in government primary schools 'levels of teaching activity were abysmally low'.[96]

There are examples of schools being closed for days on end owing to the absenteeism of teachers and heads. In the updated PROBE survey 12 per cent of government primary schools were single-teacher schools; however, an additional 21 per cent on the day of the survey were operating as single-teacher schools owing to teacher absenteeism.

Teacher activity is found wanting. Not only is there the issue of absenteeism, when teachers are present they are not necessarily teaching.

> In one instance, the head-teacher was on leave and three of the remaining five teachers who were present were standing in the playground and talking among themselves when the investigators reached the school. Some children were sitting on benches and chatting, while others were roaming around the school campus. As mentioned earlier, such instances (where schools were devoid of teaching activity at the time of the investigators' visit) were found in close to half of all schools surveyed. But there were also many schools where some teachers were teaching and some were not.

> Teaching activity is particularly limited for the very young – those enrolled in Classes 1 and 2. Instead of being given extra attention to equip them with self-confidence as they negotiate a new and alien terrain, these young children were largely ignored.[97]

The updated PROBE research found that in rural areas of Bihar 38 per cent of permanent government teachers were absent on the day of the survey. Even though facilities in rural Indian schools have improved over the last ten years (hence better teaching environments) it was found that when researchers called unannounced in around half of the government schools there was NO teaching activity going on at all,[98] exactly the same as in 1996. 'Some teachers were absent, others were found to be sipping tea, knitting, or whiling away time simply chatting'.[99] Typically parents complain about male teachers drinking during school hours (sometimes sending children to get liquor) and female teachers knitting in class.[100]

In some rural areas contractual teachers have been hired to assist permanent teachers. However, the contract teachers in some cases have been left to carry out the teaching – 'the contract teachers were certainly more active than the permanent staff' with the 'permanent teachers often' failing 'to fulfil their mandate'.[101] Some believe, and quite wrongly according to the findings of Kingdon and Aslam, that hiring contractual teachers is just a 'quick fix' because 'their limited qualifications, inadequate training and low salaries also affected the quality of their work'.[102] Rather contradictory. In fact the evidence shows that it is those who are qualified, have had adequate training and are on high salaries that have a very poor work ethic in general. That is, they do not turn up and do not teach. As mentioned, Kingdon and Aslam found that government school teachers in developing countries are typically well-qualified, have experience and are trained via a government teacher training scheme. But these criteria have little effect on student outcomes. 'Most of the standard teacher resume characteristics (such as certification and training) often used to guide education policy have no bearing on a student's standardised mark'. What seems to have more effect is that 'good private schools are ... able to retain better teachers by renewing their contracts and firing the less effective ones'.[103]

The lack of activity in government schools is seen as a 'gross injustice that is being done to Indian children today. Wasting their time day after day in idle classrooms is nothing short of a crime'.[104]

Agreed.

The reasons why government schoolteachers are typically absent have been investigated by research. Causes include lack of motivation, poor facilities in which to teach, overcrowded classrooms, government tasks to be completed on top of teaching duties, the lack of social status given to teachers, differences in caste and social status of teachers and children attending government schools, and the lack of accountability and incentives to perform.[105] But also, rural areas suffer from the lack of government teacher attendance and availability:

> Schools that are accessible may have more teachers (and also more female teachers) since teachers (and particularly female teachers) prefer to avoid postings to remote villages in the interiors. Accessible schools may also have more teachers present because these schools are more likely to be visited by education authorities.[106]

Different innovative strategies and interventions aimed at reducing teacher absenteeism in government schools in India have been tried and tested. One example by Duflo and Hanna initiated a randomised experiment in 'nonformal' single-teacher primary schools in the tribal areas of rural Udaipur district.[107] Some 60 schools were randomly selected to carry out a strategy of monitoring, using photographs taken by a camera that showed the time and date on the photo. Two photos were to be taken each day of the teacher and the class at the beginning and end of the school day, with a minimum of five hours between the photos. Teachers in the participating schools were provided a monetary incentive, which they received depending on the number of valid photos taken. They could also have money deducted as a penalty for each day missed relative to a 21-day benchmark. An additional 60 control schools did not implement the strategy. The results show that teacher absenteeism in the treatment schools dropped by half. According to the report 'the camera program was effective on two margins: it eliminated extremely delinquent behaviour (less than 50 per cent presence) and it increased the number of teachers with a perfect or very high attendance record'.[108] However, one word of warning, unofficial reports from individuals in India cast some doubt over the programme. In some cases it was said that teachers had been arriving only to take the photo; children then went home, returning for the second photo at the end of the day. These reports have not been substantiated, but bring to the fore how one has to be careful when using such strategies. It may be more beneficial to put webcams in each classroom as many private school owners do. However, this might cause an outcry from the government unions if it was tried in government schools.

Pedagogy

The updated PROBE research found that the typical pedagogical practice in government schools in India is to use rote learning. That is, 'reading' without looking at the text in the book (that is, memorisation of text as opposed to reading). Therefore pupils do not acquire the ability to read anything outside of the textbook. The overall conclusion is that it is 'not surprising that children learnt little in most schools ... learning achievements were very poor'.[109] When testing the children in math, reading and writing it was found that only around half the children in Class 5 could carry out a simple division sum and just over half single-digit multiplication. In one government school 62 per cent of Class 4 and 5 children could not read a 'simple story'; 80 per cent could not write an answer to a simple question. So even though 'resources have been pouring into improving the classroom experience ... the picture with regard to teaching methods being used is not encouraging'.[110] More on achievement will be discussed in Chapter 3.

And Still Aid Goes On

Irrespective of the data and issues that have been highlighted above, DfID promises that their focus in India will be on quality and learning. How is this going to be achieved? According to DfID it is not just about getting children into schools but ensuring that they 'are well taught and that what they learn improves their lives and economic opportunities'.[111] They plan to do this by teacher training, which for government school teachers who do not turn up to teach would be a total waste of money.

PAST OUTCOMES OF EDUCATION PROJECTS IN INDIA FUNDED BY AID

According to some reports, of the £388 million ($609 million) provided by the UK towards the SSA programme (Sarva Shiksha Abbiyan – Education for All), £70 million ($110 million) was 'squandered through widespread corruption and theft'.[112]

It has also been reported that £14 million of DfID aid has been stolen by Indian officials who spent the money purportedly on cars. Other allegations include 8000 colour television sets being bought for schools that were never delivered and indeed if they had been some of the schools had no electricity to run them. According to reports, 'tens of thousands of pounds were "allocated" to schools that don't even exist' and 'as a result even poor parents scrimp to send their children to private schools to escape the government run ones which receive British aid'.[113]

According to Pratham, irrespective of the doubling of India's education budget from 2004–2005 to 2009–2010 with 45 per cent being dedicated to elementary education, the 'close scrutiny of India's education system reveals a sobering truth – that this large investment has been spent poorly.' And the 'increased investments have failed to improve education outcomes' in government schools.[114] There are also strange accounts of government schools receiving grants for children's uniform provision in the state of Andhra Pradesh, with the money appearing in government school bank accounts and then being re-appropriated back to the school district account. It had been decided, part way through, for uniforms to be provided centrally rather than by the school. However students did not receive uniforms in time and therefore had to purchase their own.

Considering the future of DfID's programme funding in India, the following evidence was provided by Professor Anil Sadgopal from Delhi University during a Select Committee in March 2011 that 'DFID's contribution to such a national programme is not substantial enough to be necessary, or to arrest the deficiency in the Government of India's investment in education over the last twenty years'. He goes on to say:

> I think the public in Britain, the ordinary people of Britain, should ask their government, 'Why are you funding such a low quality programme in India out of the public exchequer?'[115]

Why does Sadgopal have this opinion? According to Sadgopal, in order to measure the impact of SSA and to validate the money being provided for the programme, DfID is:

funding NGOs [non-governmental organisations] to measure the ability to read only one sentence ... In school education, your whole assessment in Class 8 or Class 5 is now reduced to reading one sentence, or doing some simple two digit multiplication. You are paying NGOs to measure this and they are coming out with results that show the situation is very bad, even with respect to these parameters. So, I do not know what your government means when it says, 'Sarva Shiksah Abhiyan is proving to be very effective and remarkable progress is being made'. What criteria do they use to judge progress? I do not know.[116]

In other words, the tests that are being used to show that the SSA programme has stimulated pupils' attainment are too simplistic to illustrate any meaningful results according to this evidence provided to the Commons Select Committee.

Partly because of the failure of government programmes such as SSA, according to the Commons Select Committee documents, there has been a flourishing of low-cost private schools:

As programmes such as the Sarva Shiksha Abhiyan continue it seems more and more parents are sending their children to low fee charging private schools. We were talking to a group of parents in a fairly low income area and they were sending their children to private schools, although they said in the past everyone went to government schools. How has this trend developed? Where there has been a deterioration in the quality of the vast proportion of the government school system, it is very easy to understand that poor parents, out of desperation, will look for private schooling. And private schooling has mushroomed in India in the past ten years, precisely because the government school system had declined in quality.

One could therefore ascertain that in a way, DfID's funding of SSA is causing parents to choose low-cost private schools! The evidence suggests, as considered in Chapter 3, that is the result they should have been aiming for all along.

SSA has partly contributed to the deterioration of government schools because it has promoted 'inadequate schooling for poor children, producing educational facilities the government is too ashamed to even call schools'.[117] The evidence provided at the Select Committee goes on to suggest that 'as the quality deteriorates within it, not only is private schooling coming up, but the government is starting different layers of high quality schooling outside Sarva Shiksha Abhiyan'.[118]

And the PAISA 2011 report states that 'SSA has promoted a bottom up delivery system with no bottom up control or decision making power. The result is thus a de facto centralised top down system'.[119] Just as others have shown, the report indicates that there has been an expansion of government school provision, the 'evidence thus far suggests that education infrastructure is yet to translate into children acquiring basic abilities in reading and arithmetic'.[120] Children's outcomes have typically remained 'stagnant' since 2005. It really does not matter how much the infrastructure improves if teachers are absent or if they are in school, they just do not teach. It really is not a surprise that children's achievement is not improving.

During the Select Committee interviews other examples of misappropriation of aid money specifically given to the SSA programme were given by Dr Niranjan Aradhya, Programme Head of the Centre for Child and the Law at the National Law School of India, who described SSA as 'a colossal failure'.

> The Sarva Shiksha Abhiyan is giving money for toilet construction but they cannot provide water so after two months the toilet is useless and the children cannot use it. They think the toilet they have constructed is functional, but after inauguration, after a week there is no water. At least provide water! If you look at the Sarva Shiksha Abhiyan from this angle I don't think it has really done anything for quality education. Even today quality is a very big challenge in government schools and if you look at the overall performance of the Sarva Shiksha Abhiyan, both in terms of its mission and in terms of its progress, I personally feel it's been a colossal failure, in the sense that it has failed to achieve not only the targets, but also to bring a visible change in the school education system.[121]

Such a waste of aid.

FINAL THOUGHT

Developed country governments are being asked to increase their aid budgets in order to improve the lives of the world's poorest. However, in order to maintain public support for international development aid, governments need to look at ways to minimise waste, corruption and theft, and increase the effectiveness of aid. This chapter has set out evidence that implies that money provided to improve government schools in India might not be being used in the most efficient way nor having the desired effect; that is, improving access and pupil achievement. The main reasons for this are the inactivity of government schoolteachers, the Planners deciding where money should or needs to be directed rather than the Searchers, and Hippos happily receiving the money to maximise their own bureaus or their own pockets. If providing aid is one answer to improving children's educational opportunities and outcomes there may be a better way to allocate aid.

What is really important is the need to ask the poor what they want, use gold standard research to inform decisions and think radically about changing the way aid money is directed and transferred to the poorest. Low-cost private schools have been mushrooming in developing countries around the world, not only in urban but rural areas too. India is no exception. So how many low-cost private schools are there? What do they look like? Who goes to these schools? Is the low-cost private schools' space something the international aid agencies should be looking towards for a more effective and efficient outcome for their spending? Or does throwing money at a market that is already up and running have disaster written all over it? The following chapters therefore examine the low-cost private schools' market in India and then go on to discuss if it is possible or even desirable to enhance the sector using development aid.

NOTES

1. Kunz (1997).
2. Snowdon (2009).
3. Pearson (1969); and Brandt (1980).
4. Rawls (1971).
5. http://www.dfid.gov.uk/News/Latest-news/2010/
   UK-to-increase-aid-money-spent-on-conflict-countries1/.
6. US National Security Strategy (2010), p. 33, http://www.whitehouse.gov/sites/default/
   files/rss_viewer/national security_strategy.pdf.
7. Ibid., p. 15.
8. Moyo (2010), p. 8.
9. http://www.un.org/millenniumgoals/bkgd.shtml; see also Sachs (2001).
10. UN (2011), p. 4.
11. Sachs (2005).
12. Snowdon (2005), p. 40.
13. Das et al. (2006), p. 2.
14. £1 = $1.57.
15. See for example OECD statistics, at: http://stats.oecd.org/Index.aspx?datasetcode=
    TABLE1.
16. See Dollar and Kraay (2002; 2004).
17. Snowdon (2009), p. 258.
18. Moyo (2010), p. 37.
19. Ibid., p. xix.
20. Boone (1995).
21. Moyo (2010).
22. Acemoglu and Robinson (2012).
23. Moyo (2010); and Ayittey (2005).
24. Moyo (2010), p. 28.
25. Snowdon (2007), p. 137.
26. Hanlon et al. (2010), p. 8.
27. Chenery (1964).
28. Riddell (2008), p. 358.
29. Ibid.
30. Friedman (1958); Bauer (1976).
31. Snowdon (2005), p. 22.
32. Collier (2007), p. 99.
33. Ibid., p. 183

34. Ibid., p. 190.
35. Easterly (2006); Ayittey (2005), for example.
36. Easterly (2006), p. 6.
37. Friedman (1958), p. 509.
38. Friedman (1962), p. 146.
39. Ibid., p. 149.
40. Hayek (1945), p. 527.
41. Banerjee (2007).
42. Ayittey (2005), p. 389.
43. Sachs (2005).
44. Ayittey (2005), p. 171.
45. Prahalad (2005), p. 1.
46. http://www.dfid.gov.uk/News/Speeches-and-statements/2012/
     Andrew-Mitchell-our-aid-programme-in-India/.
47. See the *Times of India*, http://timesofindia.indiatimes.com/business/india-business/
     Crisil-pegs-economic-growth-for-2012-13-at-6-5/articleshow/13830658.cms.
48. PPP – Purchasing Power Parity.
49. UNDP (2011).
50. http://www.dfid.gov.uk/Where-we-work/Asia-South/India/.
51. Colclough with Lewin (1993).
52. Colclough and De (2010), p. 6.
53. Ibid., pp. 23–4.
54. Sachs (2005), p. 211.
55. Ibid.
56. See http://mdgs.un.org/unsd/mdg/Host.aspx?Content=indicators/officiallist.htm.
57. UN (2011), p. 17.
58. Tooley et al. (2005).
59. See for example Andrabi et al. (2010); Aslam and Kingdon (2007); Tooley et al. (2010).
60. See Chapter 3 for data on teacher attendance and lethargy in government schools.
61. http://www.dfid.gov.uk/Documents/publications1/op/india-2011-summary.pdf.
62. http://www.dfid.gov.uk/Where-we-work/Asia-South/India/.
63. DfID (2011), p. 12.
64. http://www.bicusa.org/en/Article.12629.aspx.
65. http://web.worldbank.org/WBSITE/EXTERNAL/TOPICS/EXTEDUCATION/0,,
     contentMDK:23150303~menuPK:282423~pagePK:64020865~piPK:149114~theSite
     PK:282386,00.html.
66. http://web.worldbank.org/WBSITE/EXTERNAL/NEWS/0,,contentMDK:23215107
     ~pagePK:34370~piPK:42770~theSitePK:4607,00.html.
67. Ibid., n. 21.
68. Sachs (2005), p. 3.
69. Sachs (2008), p. 4.
70. Sachs (2005), p. 254.
71. Ibid.
72. Ibid., p. 294.
73. Sachs (2008), p. 7.
74. UNESCO (2008), pp. 131 and 132.
75. Ibid., p. 164.
76. Ibid., p. 16.
77. Ibid., p. 21, emphasis added.
78. Lewin (2007), p. 44; see also Härmä (2009), p. 164.
79. Woodhead et al. (2013, in press).
80. Ibid., final page.
81. Ibid., p. 8.
82. Shiva Kumar et al. (2009), http://www.frontlineonnet.com/fl2606/stories/20090327260
     608800.htm.

83. Ibid.
84. Ibid.
85. Ibid.
86. Watkins (2011).
87. Hayek (1960), p. 122.
88. UNESCO figures available at: http://stats.uis.unesco.org/unesco/TableViewer/document.aspx?ReportId=121&IF_Language=eng&BR_Country=3560&BR_Region=40535.
89. 1 crore Rs. = 10 million Rs. = 100 lakh Rs.
90. Exchange rate at 55.85 Rs. = US$1.
91. Pratham (2011).
92. Shiva Kumar et al. (2009).
93. Ibid.
94. De et al. (2011), p. 33.
95. Kremer et al. (2005).
96. Shiva Kumar et al. (2009).
97. Ibid.
98. De et al. (2011), p. 35.
99. Ibid.
100. Ibid., p. 55.
101. Shiva Kumar et al. (2009).
102. Ibid.
103. Both quotes are from Aslam and Kingdon (2007), p. 14.
104. Shiva Kumar et al. (2009).
105. Govindu (2005); Mooij (2008); Ramachandran et al. (2005); Narayan (2007).
106. De et al. (2011), p. 22.
107. Duflo and Hanna (2005).
108. Ibid., p. 3.
109. Shiva Kumar et al. (2009).
110. De et al. (2011), pp. 37–8.
111. DfID (2011), p. 13.
112. Early Day Motion – 230, at: http://www.parliament.uk/edm/2010-12/230.
113. Sue Reid, *Daily Mail* online (2011), at: www.dailymail.co.uk/news/article-2068930/How-India-squanders-British-aid--1-4bn-country-space-programme.html.
114. Pratham (2011), p. 11.
115. Commons Select Committee March 2011, http://www.publications.parliament.uk/pa/cm201011/cmselect/cmintdev/writev/616/m07.htm.
116. Sue Reid, *Daily Mail* online (2011), at: www.dailymail.co.uk/news/article-2068930/How-India-squanders-British-aid--1-4bn-country-space-programme.html.
117. Pratham (2010), p. 11.
118. Commons Select Committee March 2011, http://www.publications.parliament.uk/pa/cm201011/cmselect/cmintdev/writev/616/m07.htm.
119. PAISA (2011), p. 7.
120. Ibid.
121. Commons Select Committee March 2011, http://www.publications.parliament.uk/pa/cm201011/cmselect/cmintdev/writev/616/m07.htm.

3 The parting of the veil – low-cost private schools – the evidence

THE EXISTENCE OF LOW-COST PRIVATE SCHOOLS

The existence of a low-cost private education sector in India is now widely acknowledged. According to one report 'a lower cost private sector has emerged to meet the demands of poor households'[1] and another that the 'failure of public school in terms of meeting parents' expectations/ aspirations' has led to a 'growing demand' for private schools in India.[2] Research carried out in villages in four north Indian states reports that 'even among poor families and disadvantaged communities, one finds parents who make great sacrifices to send some or all of their children to private schools, so disillusioned are they with government schools'.[3] Reporting on evidence from Haryana, Uttar Pradesh and Rajasthan 'private schools have been expanding rapidly in recent years' and these 'now include a large number of primary schools which charge low fees', in urban as well as rural areas.[4] For the poor in Calcutta (Kolkata) there has been a 'mushrooming of privately managed unregulated ... primary schools'[5] and in Haryana private unrecognised schools 'are operating practically in every locality of the urban centres as well as in rural areas, often located adjacent to a government school'.[6]

These schools are not fly by night. Around 20 years ago in Pakistan, Harold Alderman et al. found a high share of children enrolled in private schools. The study gained information from 1650 households in Lahore and these households were divided into six income groups. The percentage of children found in private, government or no school for each income was noted. It was found that 'a high share of children are enrolled in private schools, even children from the poorest families'.[7] In almost all of the income groups, the share of children in private schools is greater than in government schools (Table 3.1). At the time Rs. 3,500 equated to around $100, and therefore this income group was estimated to be living on less than $1 per person, per day. Even in the lowest income category government school enrolment is only slightly higher than private school enrolment (40 per cent for boys and girls in the government sector and 37 per cent for boys and girls in the private sector).

Table 3.1   *School enrolment by income group (%) in 1650 households in low-income districts in Lahore, Pakistan*

	No school			Private school			Government school		
	% of all households in group								
Income group (Rs per month)	Boys	Girls	All	Boys	Girls	All	Boys	Girls	All
< Rs. 2000/-	25%	21%	23%	35%	37%	37%	40%	41%	40%
2000–3500	5%	4%	4%	59%	52%	56%	36%	45%	40%
3500–5000	1%	1%	1%	78%	66%	72%	21%	33%	27%
5000–7000	0	0	0	84%	65%	73%	17%	35%	26%
7000–10000	0	0	0	88%	72%	79%	13%	28%	21%
> Rs. 10,000/-	0	0	0	88%	81%	84%	12%	19%	16%
All	11%	8%	10%	61%	55%	58%	28%	37%	32%

Source: Alderman et al. (1996), Table 1.A., p. 23.

Looking at household survey data, between 1991 and 1996 the percentage of children enrolled in private schools in the urban Punjab, including Lahore, increased by 8 percentage points. In Sindh province (with its capital Karachi, south of the Punjab and bordering the Indian states of Gujarat and Rajasthan) the increase was even higher at 18 percentage points.[8] Data on private unaided school numbers or enrolments was not recorded in any provincial government databases at the time.

It is estimated that today in Pakistan there are more than 47,000 private schools catering to about one-third of primary school enrolees.[9]

Again providing evidence of the longevity of low-cost private schools, research undertaken by Yash Aggarwal in 1999 surveyed 495 villages/urban towns in Haryana, India. Researchers visited every private primary school they came across whether it appeared on a government list or not. Data were collected from 878 private unaided unrecognised primary schools, and 1242 private unaided recognised primary schools located in the survey area. Aggarwal believed that the choice for parents was no longer whether to send their children to school but to 'which type of school' they should be sent.[10] Almost 14 years ago the estimate was that in Haryana almost 50 per cent of children who were attending primary schools were enrolled in the private sector, many from low-income families.

So why the mushrooming of private unaided schools and what does the sector look like today?

WHY THE MUSHROOMING

One reason given for this 'mushrooming' of private schools in India is that they provide English-medium instruction, desired by parents; government schools teach in state languages, not usually teaching English until about Class 5.[11] Being able to converse in English raises potential earnings. Some studies have shown that being fluent in English implies hourly wages 34 per cent higher than for those who speak no English, and this is after controlling for levels of education and personal characteristics.[12] The economic return for being fluent in English has been estimated to be equivalent to the return for completing a secondary education. Other reasons for the 'mushrooming' highlight the low quality of government schools,[13] some of which have been explored in Chapter 2, including problems of teacher absenteeism, lack of teacher commitment and inadequate conditions. In government primary schools in West Bengal it is reported that 'teachers do not teach' and 'teaching is the last priority for the teachers'[14]; in some rural areas of India in only 53 per cent of government schools was there any teaching going on at all.[15] Indeed, poor households often state that it is teacher absenteeism in the state sector that made them choose to send their children to private schools.[16] A comprehensive survey of teacher absenteeism conducted by the World Bank in India found absenteeism rates of 25.2 per cent in rural and 22.9 per cent in urban government schools.[17]

Conditions in government schools in Bihar have been described as 'horrific',[18] with facilities in government primary schools in Calcutta reported as 'by no means satisfactory', often operating without safe drinking water or toilets.[19] The Probe Team in India found that out of 162 government primary schools, 59 per cent had no functional water supply, 89 per cent had no toilets, and only 23 per cent had a library, and 48 per cent a playground. The average pupil–teacher ratio was 68:1. According to research carried out in eight India states:

> uniformly, whether it was the quality of school building, one-classroom schools, drinking water or toilets for staff and students (especially girls), government schools come out looking worse than private unaided ones ... there are fewer school working days in government schools ... the drop-out rates are higher and the attendance rates lower in all States in government schools than for private unaided schools.[20]

Concerns are equally expressed about the quality of the private schools to which parents turn as alternatives, especially those not recognised by government. Such schools are purportedly of 'inferior quality', offering 'a low-quality service' that will 'restrict children's future opportunities'.[21] And in Calcutta, 'the mushrooming of privately managed unregulated

pre-primary and primary schools ... can have only deleterious consequences for the spread of education in general and among the poor in
particular'.[22]

However, the evidence given about poor quality private provision
and the relative quality of public and private provision for the poor in
these sources is limited. Indeed it is suggested that 'little hard evidence' is
available.[23] The studies presented here aimed to contribute to the understanding of such private school provision, and its relative quality vis-à-vis
government delivery.

In India there are three school management types – private unaided
(PUA), private aided (PA) and government (G). PUA schools can be recognised or unrecognised and are privately managed and funded typically
only by school fees paid by parents. Recognition status implies that the
private school purportedly abides by the on-paper laws and rules as set
out in the education acts of the state. Unrecognised schools have yet to
obtain that status, sometimes by choice, and are in effect operating in the
extra legal sector. It can take some time for recognition to be granted to a
school, especially if bribes from the school entrepreneur are not forthcoming or inadequate for the application to be chivvied along through the
bureaucratic process.

Why would schools want to become recognised? Recognised status allows
schools to provide transfer certificates for their pupils as well as to facilitate
the taking of state examinations. Also, one is less likely to be closed down
if one has been 'seen' to fulfil the requirements. Indeed the recent Right to
Education Act (2010) sets out that the closure of unrecognised schools will
begin if recognition status has not been reached within three years of the
Act. PA schools are in the minority in India, but are privately managed
with teacher salaries funded by the government; hence they are more government type schools than private and hence experience similar problems.
Government schools are those provided and funded by the state. So what
does the research show about these different school management types and
what do we know about low-cost private schools in India?

NUMBER OF SCHOOLS AND PUPIL ENROLMENT

Census and surveys of urban and rural areas where poor parents reside
have been carried out around India in order to try to assess how large the
low-cost private school network actually is. Researchers are trained in
methods to allow them to locate schools that are not on government lists
owing to their lack of recognition status and thus are operating under the
radar of most agencies as well as the Indian government. This typically

includes going into market places and asking at stationery stores where the local schools are located. Other techniques included watching for children with uniforms making their way to and from school and enquiring from mothers shopping at market stalls where they send their children to school. Maps have been produced of the research areas to allow the plotting of schools once found. Researchers plot the schools to ensure that every street and alleyway has been covered by the team, with primary and secondary schools being the main focus and nursery only schools or informal education typically excluded.

According to Anuradha De et al. and a survey to update the initial Public Report on Basic Education in India (PROBE), over the ten years from 1996–2006, in rural India, there has been a 'massive growth in the availability of private schools'.[24] Thousands of private schools have 'sprung up' in every state, where at least one in three villages had a private school. In urban settings private schools can account for 60–80 per cent of schools. Karthik Muralidharan and Michael Kremer looked at the existence of private schools in village settings in 20 states in India, representing 98 per cent of the population. Their data show that private schools were significantly more likely to be in villages with high teacher absence in government schools and with larger populations. Interestingly, in states with higher per capita income it was less likely that there would be private schools in their villages.[25]

There have been a number of research projects that have specifically carried out a census in low-income areas, just as in the time of Munro and Macaulay. Table 3.2 shows the numbers of schools in their different management categories located in low-income areas of Hyderabad, Delhi, Patna and Mahbubnagar.

In the notified slum areas[26] of three zones of the Old City of Hyderabad – Charminar, Bandlaguda and Bhadurpura – totalling an area of 19 square miles, 918 schools in total were located. As shown in Table 3.2, of these just over one-third are government, with roughly the same number of low-cost PUA unrecognised schools as government schools. Around one-quarter is PUA recognised schools. As with all of these results it should be pointed out that it is difficult to assess whether all PUA unrecognised schools have been located as there are no official lists or figures with which to compare the findings. Hence the number found represents a lower bound of unrecognised schools in each location. North Shahdara in east Delhi covers an area of around 40 km²; the designated slum area takes up about half of this total space. Two hundred and sixty-five schools were located, with over two-thirds being PUA schools. Again, as in the Hyderabad study, there are more unrecognised private schools than government schools.

Table 3.2   Number of schools

School type	Hyderabad		Delhi		Patna		Mahbubnagar	
	Number	%	Number	%	Number	%	Number	%
Government	320	34.9	71	26.8	336	21	384	62.4
Private aided	49	5.3	19	7.2	14	1	11	1.8
Private unaided unrecognised	335	36.5	73	27.5	1224	78	77	12.5
Private unaided recognised	214	23.3	102	38.5	0	0	143	23.3
Total	918	100.0	265	100.0	1574	100	615	100.0

Source: Tooley et al. (2007); Tooley and Dixon (2007); Rangaraju et al. (2012).

In Patna, Bihar, every PUA school was visited within the Patna urban area. Government 'official' data were used for government school statistics. In Patna 1224 PUA schools were visited. In the same vicinity were 336 government schools. The total number of schools in Patna Urban was found to be 1574. PUA schools make up the vast majority of schools in Patna – 78 per cent, compared to only 21 per cent of government schools. Because Patna was a slightly different study, in that PUA schools were visited irrespective of whether they were in a slum or low-income area, it was decided to divide them into three categories, related to their maximum monthly fees charged, in order to determine how many were 'low-cost'. Low-cost private schools had a maximum monthly fee of less than Rs. 300 ($5.37), the school was classified 'affordable' if the maximum monthly fee ranged between Rs. 300 ($5.37) and Rs. 499 ($8.93), and finally higher cost schools were charging a maximum monthly fee of Rs. 500 ($8.95) or over. Using this categorisation, and from the 1000 schools answering the question regarding school fees, 69.1 per cent of PUA schools are low-cost, 22.3 per cent are affordable, and only 8.6 per cent are higher cost. That is, the vast majority of PUA schools found in urban Patna are low-cost, charging less than Rs. 300/- ($5.37) per month. In Mahbubnagar, Andhra Pradesh, 615 schools were located in five mandals (sub-districts), four being rural and one urban. Of these, 62.4 per cent are government and 35.8 per cent PUA schools. Of the PUA schools, 143 are recognised and 77 unrecognised.

The majority of government schools located in the low-income and slum areas of Hyderabad, Delhi and Mahbubnagar are typically primary only schools. Between 10 per cent and 17 per cent of government schools provide primary and secondary sections. Hyderabad is very different from Delhi, where around three-quarters of private recognised schools typically

Table 3.3   Mahbubnagar, age of schools

	Age of school					
	1 to 5 years old	6 to 10 years old	11 to 15 years old	16 to 20 years old	greater than 20 years old	Total
Government	69	56	18	23	202	368
	18.8%	15.2%	4.9%	6.3%	54.9%	100.0%
Private aided					11	11
					100.0%	100.0%
Private unaided unrecognised	47	11	12	3	3	76
	61.8%	14.5%	15.8%	3.9%	3.9%	100.0%
Private unaided recognised	15	32	31	13	21	112
	13.4%	28.6%	27.7%	11.6%	18.8%	100.0%
Total	131	99	61	39	237	567
	23.1%	17.5%	10.8%	6.9%	41.8%	100.0%

Source: Dixon et al. (2009), Working Paper.

are all through schools, catering for all sections, compared to Delhi where fewer than 10 per cent supply education for all grades. In Mahbubnagar around a quarter of recognised schools serve all sections.

These PUA schools are clearly not 'fly by night' as some of the literature suggests. In Hyderabad the mean year of establishment for unrecognised schools was seven years. Recognised schools had been established for an average of 17 years. In Delhi unrecognised schools on average had been established for six years and recognised schools 11 years. In Mahbubnagar a total of 47 (61.8 per cent) unrecognised private schools had been opened within the last five years, compared to only 15 (13.4 per cent) of recognised private schools. However, while unrecognised schools are certainly newer than their recognised counterparts, a significant minority have been running for more than five years. Many government primary schools have also been created recently (18.8 per cent), likely to have been under the Sarva Shiksha Abhiyan and World Bank DPEP programmes (see Table 3.3).[27]

In Patna, private schools seem to have been running for many years and in some cases even decades. Data collected in 2011 show the mean year of establishment for the recognised private schools to be 1987, while for the unrecognised schools it was 1997. Table 3.4 shows the data by recognition status and affordability of the schools. It turns out that the reported oldest school was an unrecognised low-cost private school founded in 1937! The median date for opening of an unrecognised low-cost private school was 2000, compared to 1982 for a recognised low-cost private school.

Table 3.4 Year of establishment of the private schools in Patna

Year of establishment, recognition and affordability

Recognition status	Affordability of the school	N	Mean	Standard deviation	Minimum	Maximum	Range	Median
Recognised	Low-cost private school	16	1983	15.5	1961	2006	45	1982
	Affordable private school	9	1986	16.8	1959	2008	49	1986
	Higher cost private school	15	1992	11.4	1965	2007	42	1994
	Total	40	1987	14.6	1959	2008	49	1991
Unrecognised	Low-cost private school	672	1997	10.9	1937	2011	74	2000
	Affordable private school	214	1999	9.8	1950	2011	61	2001
	Higher cost private school	68	1995	12.3	1960	2010	50	1998
	Total	954	1997	10.8	1937	2011	74	2000
NOC	Low-cost private school	1	1954		1954	1954	0	1954
	Higher cost private school	3	1991	9.0	1981	1997	16	1996
	Total	4	1982	20.0	1954	1997	43	1989
Total	Low-cost private school	689	1996	11.3	1937	2011	74	1999
	Affordable private school	223	1998	10.4	1950	2011	61	2001
	Higher cost private school	86	1994	12.0	1960	2010	50	1996
	Total	998	1996	11.2	1937	2011	74	2000

Source: Rangaraju et al. (2012).

What proportion of children is enrolled in low-cost private schools in India? In rural India, it is estimated, 24 per cent of children aged 6–14 are enrolled in private schools, and in the states of Haryana, Kerala, Manipur and Meghalaya the share probably exceeds 40 per cent.[28] In urban areas the figures are much higher.

In the low-income areas of the three zones of Hyderabad a total of 262,075 children attended the 918 schools, with 65 per cent of them in low-cost PUA schools (see Table 3.5). There is roughly the same number of children attending PUA unrecognised schools as government schools.

There is a similar story for Mahbubnagar. In Mahbubnagar's 615 schools it was reported that 122,262 children were enrolled at the time of the census. Breaking this down by management type, there were slightly more children enrolled in PUA schools than government schools – 48.2 per cent compared to 47.8 per cent. For the PUA sector, 41.6 per cent of total children were in recognised schools, while 6.6 per cent were in unrecognised schools.

Disaggregating into rural and urban areas, a majority of schoolchildren were in government schools in the rural areas (74.1 per cent). In the 'small town' urban areas, these figures are reversed – with only 26.2 per cent of schoolchildren in government schools and 66.7 per cent in PUA schools (see Table 3.6).

With regard to Patna, government data were provided for government and PA schools, and the research data from 1000 PUA schools were extrapolated to the 1224 PUA schools found by the survey teams. Sixty-five per cent of schoolchildren in Patna attend PUA schools, with just 34 per cent attending government schools. In other words, roughly two out of three schoolchildren in urban Patna attend a PUA school, either low-cost affordable or higher cost.

Breaking down this data further to look at the different categories of PUA schools shows that there are virtually as many children in low-cost private schools as there are government schools – 32 per cent for PUA low-cost and 34 per cent for government schools (see Table 3.7). Or to put it another way, nearly one out of three children in urban Patna attend a low-cost private school charging fees less than Rs. 300 ($5.37) per month.

There is one anomaly in the data, and that is from Delhi. In the 265 schools located in the low-income and slum areas of Shahdara there were in total 137,493 children. Of these, 60.4 per cent were in government schools, 3.7 per cent in PA, 27.2 per cent in recognised PUA schools and finally 8.8 per cent in unrecognised PUA schools. This is very different from other studies in urban low-income areas, with 36 per cent of enrolment being in PUA schools.

Three caveats must be made about this reported enrolment. First, there

Table 3.5 Pupil enrolment by management type and location

Management type	Hyderabad		Delhi		Patna		Mahbubnagar	
	No. children	% of total	No. children	% of total	No. children	% of total	No. children	% of total
Government	62,839	24.0	82,994	60.4	91,087	33.9	58,482	47.8
Private aided	29,976	11.4	5108	3.7	3925	1.5	4786	3.9
Private unaided unrecognised	60,533	23.1	12,038	8.8	173,491	64.6	8100	6.6
Private unaided recognised	108,727	41.5	37,353	27.2			50,894	41.6
Total	262,075	100	137,493	100	268,503	100	122,262	100

Source: Tooley et al. (2007); Tooley and Dixon (2007); Rangaraju et al. (2012).

Table 3.6 Mahbubnagar rural and urban breakdown of schools and children numbers

Urban/rural	Management type	Total number of children	Number of schools	Mean size of school	% of children in management type
Rural	Government	40,965	316	129.64	74.1
	Private unaided unrecognised	3811	38	100.29	6.9
	Private unaided recognised	10,539	36	292.75	19.1
	Total	55,315	390	141.83	100.0
Urban	Government	17,517	68	257.60	26.2
	Private aided	4786	11	435.09	7.1
	Private unaided unrecognised	4289	39	109.97	6.4
	Private unaided recognised	40,355	107	377.15	60.3
	Total	66,947	225	297.54	100.0
Total	Government	58,482	384	152.30	47.8
	Private aided	4786	11	435.09	3.9
	Private unaided unrecognised	8100	77	105.19	6.6
	Private unaided recognised	50,894	143	355.90	41.6
	Total	122,262	615	198.80	100.0

Source: Dixon et al. (2009).

*Table 3.7   Enrolment by school management type, including affordability
of PUA schools*

School type		Enrolment	% of total	% of private unaided	% of total
Government		91,087	33.9		33.9
Private aided		3925	1.5		1.5
Private unaided		173,491	64.6		
	Low-cost	85,515		49.3	31.8
	Affordable	46,348		26.7	17.3
	Higher cost	41,628		24.0	15.5
Total		268,503			100.0

Source: Rangaraju et al. (2012).

is the reported propensity of government and PA schools to exaggerate enrolment, with clear financial and job security incentives to claim larger enrolment than is actually the case.[29] Second, it was reported anecdotally that there may be some double-enrolment of children in both government and private schools, for this enabled a child to attend private school during the morning and government school for the free lunch provided; also, it would enable a child to take state examinations and gain transfer certificates, which would not be possible in an unrecognised private school. Third, we have no way of checking that the researchers located all unrecognised schools. For each of these reasons, it is suggested that the data here may be an underestimate of the true proportion of enrolment in PUA schools, especially unrecognised schools.

It is often assumed that parents choose boys over girls to attend low-cost private schools. Research has therefore been carried out to see if this is the case. Table 3.8 shows some of the findings on gender distribution in the different school management types.

In Hyderabad and Delhi there is a higher percentage of girls in school than boys. In Mahbubnagar a slightly higher percentage of boys is reported in school. More girls attended private unrecognised schools in Hyderabad, but taking both recognised and unrecognised schools together there is almost an equal number of boys and girls in private schools. In Delhi a greater number of girls are in government schools but more boys attend private schools at around 57 per cent. In Mahbubnagar, overall, government schools had rough parity in the ratio of boys and girls, but more boys are attending private schools. In Patna figures show that 53.8 per cent of students in government schools are girls, compared to 43.4 per cent of girls in private schools. Disaggregated we see that 45 per cent of

Table 3.8 Enrolment and gender

Management type	Hyderabad		Delhi		Patna		Mahbubnagar	
	Numbers reported	% enrolled	Numbers reported	% enrolled	Numbers reported	% enrolled	Numbers reported	% enrolled
Government								
Boys	26,897	42.8	32,846	39.6	42,082	46.2	29,007	49.6
Girls	35,942	57.2	50,148	60.4	49,005	53.8	29,475	50.4
Private aided								
Boys	12,907	43.1	2848	55.8			2470	51.6
Girls	17,069	56.9	2260	44.2			2316	48.4
PUA unrecognised								
Boys	29,183	48.2	6926	57.5	130,014	56.6	4576	56.5
Girls	31,350	51.8	5112	42.5	99,636	43.4	3524	43.5
PUA recognised								
Boys	54,926	50.5	21,272	56.9			28,348	55.7
Girls	53,801	49.5	16,081	43.1			22,546	44.3
Total								
Boys	123,913	47.3	63,892	46.5			63,209	51.7
Girls	138,162	52.7	73,601	53.5			59,053	48.3

Source: Tooley et al. (2007); Tooley and Dixon (2007); Rangaraju et al. (2012).

students in Patna in the low-cost private schools are girls, with 41 per cent in affordable and 42 per cent in higher cost private schools.

Looking at the figures they seem not to be skewed completely one way or the other. The data seem to dispel worries that boys are chosen to attend private schools over girls. It is interesting in the Old City of Hyderabad where the majority of families are Muslim that there is almost equal parity of gender in private schools.

REASONS FOR CHOOSING LOW-COST PRIVATE SCHOOLS

So why are parents choosing to pay for schooling when government education is supposedly free? In some cases parents prefer English-medium schools, typically class sizes are smaller in private schools, teacher activity is greater and facilities are typically better. Evidence on each of these elements is provided below.

Medium of Instruction

One of the main reasons provided for parents choosing PUA schools over and above government ones is that they provide instruction in English;[30] that is, they are English-medium schools. It is certainly the case that there is a significant difference between government and private schools and their medium of instruction. In Hyderabad a large majority of private recognised (87.8 per cent) and unrecognised (80.2 per cent) schools reported they were English-medium. For government schools the same figure was tiny, at 0.6 per cent. Government schools in Hyderabad were typically Urdu-medium (72.6 per cent).

In Delhi and Mahbubnagar, fewer private schools were English-medium; however, there were significantly more than government schools. In Delhi, 47.1 per cent of recognised and 20.5 per cent of unrecognised schools reported they were English-medium compared to 2.8 per cent of government schools. The majority of government schools were Hindi-medium (80.3 per cent). Many of the unrecognised schools also stated that they were Hindi-medium or ran both Hindi and English streams. Only three government schools in Mahbubnagar were English-medium compared to around half of the private schools. Government schools taught in either Urdu or Telugu. Again around half of the low-cost private schools in Patna are English-medium only, with many of them offering English and Hindi.

Table 3.9   Patna pupil–teacher measure

	Number of teachers	Number of pupils	Number of pupils/ number of teachers	Number of schools
Government	2151	91,087	42.3	336
Private unaided	10,379	229,650	22.1	1000
Low-cost	5519	116,010	21.0	691
Affordable	2860	61,325	21.4	223
Higher cost	2000	52,315	26.2	86

Source: Rangaraju et al. (2012).

Teachers and Students

Typically, class sizes are much larger in government schools than in private schools. Government school class sizes are generally at least double that of low-cost private schools. The data from Patna are typical, showing that for PUA the pupil–teacher ratio is 22.1 pupils per teacher, compared to 42.3 in the government schools. Interestingly, the low-cost private schools have the lowest pupil–teacher ratio of all, at 21.0 pupils per teacher (see Table 3.9).

School Facilities and Teaching Activity

Surveys of inputs have compared the teaching activity and facilities across the different school management types. The majority of these indicators are regarded as important proxies for the quality of the learning experience, such as those vital for basic health and hygiene (for example, drinking water and toilets), for safety, comfort and ease of learning (for example, 'pucca' buildings, electricity in the classroom, fans, desks, chairs and blackboards). Other indicators focused on inputs signalling investment in educational provision (library, tape recorders, television and computers for teaching purposes). The findings regarding each will be considered in turn.

Teacher activity

As already discussed in Chapter 2, various studies have found evidence of teacher negligence, especially in government schools. A study by Michael Kremer and his team found that making unannounced visits to 3700 schools in 20 states in India on average revealed that one-quarter of government primary schoolteachers was absent on any one day. Of those who were present only around half were actually teaching. The PROBE team have reported similar findings on two separate occasions a decade apart, and the ASER (Assessment Survey Evaluation Research) 2011 report finds average government schoolteacher absence to be around 13 per cent, with 65 per cent of schools operating between Class I and V having all teachers present and 52 per cent of schools operating between Class I and VIII having all teachers present on the day of the visit.[31]

During unannounced visits researchers have visited classrooms to observe, without notice, the activity of the class teacher. In each of the following examples researchers were told to visit Class 4, and where this did not operate then the nearest grade to it.

Teaching was defined when the teacher was carrying out an activity in the classroom that could be classified as teaching. This included supervising the class in an activity, supervising reading, children doing their own work, pupil-led activities and children working at the blackboard or in groups. Non-teaching activity was classified as when the teacher was not present in the classroom, but was supposed to be and the teacher was in school. This could include the teacher sitting in the staffroom, eating, sleeping, talking or chatting with other teachers or occupied in any non-teaching activity in another part of the school when they should have been engaged with their own class.

The research findings actually seem mixed with regard to absenteeism but more conclusive with regard to teaching activity (see Table 3.10).

In Hyderabad and Mahbubnagar teacher absenteeism is lower in PUA schools than in government schools. In Delhi, government schools had fewer teachers absent, but of those present more than half of them were not teaching when they were supposed to be.

The most teaching activity was found in private recognised schools in Mahbubnagar and Hyderabad, and in unrecognised schools in Delhi. In Hyderabad 74.6 per cent of government schoolteachers were teaching compared to 90.5 per cent in unrecognised and 97.5 per cent recognised schools. In Delhi, just over one-third of government teachers were teaching, with over half non-teaching. Again, in Mahbubnagar, teacher activity was lower in government than private schools: In government classes, 63.8 per cent of teachers were teaching when they were supposed to be, compared to 72.7 per cent in PA, 80.0 per cent in unrecognised PUA and 82.7 per cent in recognised PUA.

Teacher activity is much higher in PUA schools than government ones.

Although private school teachers are paid in some cases one-tenth of the government teachers in rural Uttar Pradesh (Rs. 10,860 ($194) and Rs. 8,952 ($160) per year on average for recognised and unrecognised schoolteachers compared to Rs. 100,383 ($1,797) per year for a government teacher), Joanna Härmä observes 'substantive differences' in teaching

Table 3.10 *Teacher activity and absenteeism in Hyderabad, Delhi and Mahbubnagar*

	Hyderabad			Delhi			Mahbubnagar		
	Teaching	Non-teaching	Absent	Teaching	Non-teaching	Absent	Teaching	Non-teaching	Absent
Government	223	59	17	27	40	4	229	103	27
	74.6%	19.7%	5.7%	38.0%	56.3%	5.6%	63.8%	28.7%	7.5%
Private aided	43	2	0	12	5	2	8	3	
	95.6%	4.4%	0	63.2%	26.3%	10.5%	72.7%	27.3%	
PUA unrecognised	295	18	13	52	13	7	60	10	5
	90.5%	5.5%	4.0%	72.2%	18.1%	9.7%	80.0%	13.3%	6.7%
PUA recognised	192	4	1	70	23	8	91	14	5
	97.5%	2.0%	0.5%	69.3%	22.8%	7.9%	82.7%	12.7%	4.5%
Total	753	83	31	161	81	21	388	130	37
	86.9%	9.6%	3.6%	61.2%	30.8%	8.0%	69.9%	23.4%	6.7%

Source: Tooley et al. (2007); Tooley and Dixon (2007).

activity between government and private schools. Children in low-cost private schools in the villages 'were without exception ... being taught or working on exercises, while there was virtually no teaching taking place at government schools'.[32]

Other research has considered the differences in teacher salaries. In Delhi, Hyderabad and Mahbubnagar, a sample of Class 4 teachers was asked to provide information regarding their monthly salaries. The average monthly salary for a full-time teacher in a government school in Hyderabad was reported to be Rs. 4,479 ($80.20) compared to the salary of Rs. 1,223/- ($21.90) in unrecognised and Rs. 1,725 ($30.89) in recognised PUA schools. The average salary in a government school is therefore more than three and a half times higher than in an unrecognised PUA school and two and a half times higher than in a recognised PUA school. In Delhi there was a slightly different story, with government school-teachers in Class 5 earning on average Rs. 10,072 ($180.34) compared to Rs. 1,360 ($24.35) in unrecognised and Rs. 3,627 ($64.94) in recognised PUA schools. Therefore, in this respect, government schoolteachers are earning on average seven times more than teachers in unrecognised PUA schools and two and a half times more than in recognised PUA schools. In Mahbubnagar, the mean monthly salary of teachers in government schools was reported to be Rs. 5,430/- ($97.22), compared to Rs. 821/- ($14.70) in unrecognised PUA schools and Rs. 1,698/- ($30.40) in recognised PUA schools. Again, as in the Delhi case, the average salaries in government schools are reported to be almost seven times higher than in the unrecognised PUA schools, and around three and a half times those in the recognised PUA schools.

Teacher salaries in PA and PUA schools in Patna show that the average monthly salary of teachers in low-cost private schools was Rs. 1,447/- ($25.91) per month, with a median of Rs. 1,250/- ($22.38). Affordable private schools had the same median as PA schools (Rs. 2,500/- ($44.76) per month), although a lower mean (Rs. 3,074/- ($55.04) compared to Rs. 3,525 ($63.12)). Recognised schools had in general higher monthly teacher salaries than the unrecognised.

Facilities
Typically, low-cost private schools have better facilities than government schools. The one facility where government schools often gain over private schools is the provision of playgrounds. The great numbers of schools operate in 'pucca' buildings; that is, a proper brick or stone building, as compared to a tent or on a veranda or in an open space. Data have been collected on facilities and materials in the different school management types.

Summarising the findings:

- *Drinking water for children:* The great majority of private schools have drinking water available for their pupils; however, in Hyderabad only 57.5 per cent of government schools provided drinking water for their pupils.
- *Toilets for children:* In Hyderabad and Delhi almost all private recognised and unrecognised schools provide toilets for students. However, only one half of Hyderabad government schools have student toilets (51.9 per cent) and in Delhi only 80 per cent of government schools provided toilets. Private recognised schools in Madhya Pradesh are more likely to have toilets than government schools.
- *Separate toilets for boy and girls*: Only 11.3 per cent of government schools (excluding single-sex schools) had separate toilets for boys and girls, compared to 57.9 per cent of unrecognised and 85.3 per cent of recognised PUA schools in Hyderabad. In Patna around 70 per cent of low-cost private schools had this facility. Private recognised schools are more likely to have a separate toilet for girls than government schools in Madhya Pradesh.[33]
- *Library for use by children:* The majority of schools do not have a library. However, the school management type providing the most libraries is recognised private, where almost one-third of schools had a library in Hyderabad and Delhi (32.7 per cent and 37 per cent, respectively).

  Only three government schools in Hyderabad had library provision (1 per cent).
- *Computers for children's use:* About half of the recognised private schools in Hyderabad, Delhi and Patna had one or more computers for the use of their students, compared with 13.2 per cent and 24 per cent of unrecognised private schools in Hyderabad and Delhi, respectively. Only 1.6 per cent of government schools in Hyderabad and 7 per cent in Delhi provided a computer.
- *Television:* The majority of schools do not have televisions; however, about one-third of recognised PUA schools in Hyderabad have a television for teaching purposes. Only 4.8 per cent of government schools have a television.
- *Desks:* In Hyderabad 63.3 per cent of recognised and 31.3 per cent of unrecognised PUA schools have desks available in the classroom, compared to only 1.9 per cent of government classrooms. Again, in Delhi, government schools come out worse, where 67 per cent of classrooms have desks compared to 87 per cent of private recognised and 90 per cent of private unrecognised schools.

- *Chairs or benches for children:* In Hyderabad 81.2 per cent of recognised and 70.6 per cent of unrecognised schools have chairs or benches available in the classroom, compared to 7 per cent of government schools. Again, in Delhi, almost all private schools have chairs or benches, but almost one-third of government classrooms have no chairs or benches for children.
- *Electric light:* In Hyderabad, only 11.1 per cent of government schools have electric lights available or functioning in the classroom, compared to 45.4 per cent of unrecognised private and 60.2 per cent of recognised private schools. For Delhi, around three-quarters of government schools provide electricity compared to almost all private schools. Similarly, in Madhya Pradesh and Uttar Pradesh private recognised schools are more likely to provide electricity than government schools. This was also the finding of village schools in 20 Indian states. Private schools are more likely to have an electricity connection.

Low-cost private schools, both recognised and unrecognised, are likely to provide facilities for children that are better than those in government schools. They are more likely to have teachers who are engaged in teaching in classrooms with fewer children who are sitting at desks on chairs, even when private schools are more cost-effective at least in terms of teacher salaries, which makes up a very large proportion of recurrent expenditure, estimated to be around 93 per cent in government schools in India.

THE AFFORDABILITY OF PRIVATE SCHOOLS FEES

In India PUA schools were found to charge predominantly monthly fees. Typically there is a statistically significant difference in the fees charged in unrecognised and recognised schools, with the former consistently lower than the latter, at each level. In Hyderabad, for the first grade the mean fee in recognised schools is Rs. 95.60 ($1.71) per month compared to Rs. 68.32 ($1.22) per month in the unrecognised schools (see Table 3.11). For the fourth grade the figures are Rs. 102.55 ($1.84) compared to Rs. 78.17 ($1.40). For a breadwinner on minimum wage it would cost about 4.2 per cent per month of that wage to send a child to an unrecognised school and 5.5 per cent for a recognised one.

In Delhi the mean fees for pre-primary grade in recognised private schools is Rs. 190.25 ($3.41) per month compared to Rs. 92.55 ($1.66) per month in unrecognised schools. For primary grade the figures are Rs. 227.60 ($4.08) compared with Rs. 124.45 ($2.23). In Delhi it would cost

Table 3.11   Monthly fees in Hyderabad, Delhi and Mahbubnagar

City	Pre-primary monthly		1st grade monthly		4th grade monthly	
	Recognised	Unrecognised	Recognised	Unrecognised	Recognised	Unrecognised
Hyderabad			Rs. 95.60 ($1.71)	Rs. 68.32 ($1.22)	Rs. 102.55 ($1.84)	Rs. 78.17 ($1.40)
Delhi	Rs. 190.25 ($3.41)	Rs. 92.55 ($1.66)	Rs.227.60 ($4.08)	Rs. 124.45 ($2.23)		
Mahbubnagar			Rs. 83.40/- ($1.49)	Rs. 60.00/- ($1.07)	Rs. 93.51/- ($1.67)	Rs. 68.50 ($1.23)

Source: Tooley et al. (2007); Tooley and Dixon (2007).

about 5 per cent of a minimum wage to send a child to a private unrecognised school and about 9 per cent to a recognised one.

In Mahbubnagar, for first grade, mean fees in recognised PUA schools were Rs. 83.40/- ($1.49) per month, compared to Rs. 60.00/- ($1.07) per month in unrecognised schools. At fourth grade, the same figures were Rs. 93.51/- ($1.67) compared to Rs. 68.50 ($1.23).

Private school managers were asked whether they received additional funds for recurrent or capital expenditure *in addition to those* from school fees and other income from students. The vast majority of the PUA schools reported receiving no outside funding at all. The income of the vast majority of these schools is solely made up of the school fees.

Minimum wages for Andhra Pradesh are in the range Rs. 25.96/- ($0.46) to Rs. 78.77/- ($1.41) per day.[34] Taking a low minimum wage to be Rs.26/- ($0.47) per day, this translates to about Rs. 624/- ($11.17) per month (assuming 24 working days). So, mean fees for unrecognised schools for fourth grade might be 9.1 per cent of the monthly wage for a breadwinner on the lowest minimum wage. At the highest end, a minimum wage of Rs. 78.77/- ($1.41) would translate to about Rs. 1,890.48/- ($33.85) per month. For someone on this wage, unrecognised PUA school fees at fourth grade would be about 3.6 per cent of monthly earnings, while recognised PUA fees might be about 4.9 per cent. As noted previously in Patna, we defined the PUA schools in three categories:

- low-cost means the maximum monthly fee in the school is less than Rs. 300/- ($5.37);
- affordable means the maximum monthly fee is between Rs. 300/- ($5.37) and Rs. 499/- ($8.93);
- higher cost means the maximum monthly fee is Rs. 500/- ($8.95) or over.

Table 3.12 shows other findings regarding the fee range with schools defined in this way (data were on 993 PUA and PA schools for this information). The low-cost private schools, for instance, had a minimum monthly fee of Rs. 20/- ($0.36), and a maximum of Rs. 290/- ($5.19), with a median minimum fee of Rs. 100/- ($1.79) and a median maximum of Rs. 150/- ($2.69).

Table 3.13 shows that in general in Patna recognised schools are more expensive than unrecognised ones – with a median minimum fee of Rs. 200/- ($3.58) per month, compared to Rs. 150/- ($2.69) for the unrecognised.

Irrespective of government incentives in a rural district in western Uttar Pradesh (UP) to get children to attend government schools (free

Table 3.12   Maximum and minimum fees and affordability Patna (Rs/-)

Affordability of the school		Fees in private unaided and aided schools						
		N	Mean	Standard deviation	Minimum	Maximum	Range	Median
Minimum fee	Low-cost private school	684	114	48.63	20	275	255	100
	Affordable private school	220	229	75.86	50	450	400	225
	Higher cost private school	86	432	371.28	105	2500	2395	313
	Private aided	3	120	107.59	10	225	215	125
	Total	993	167	153.79	10	2500	2490	150
Maximum fee	Low-cost private school	684	156	63.05	30	290	260	150
	Affordable private school	220	351	51.16	275	495	220	350
	Higher cost private school	86	731	460.60	500	3000	2500	588
	Private aided	3	180	181.87	15	375	360	150
	Total	993	249	223.60	15	3000	2985	200

Source: Rangaraju et al. (2012).

Table 3.13 Patna – recognition and affordability of fees (Rs/-)

Affordability of the school		Recognition and fees, private and unaided schools only						
		N	Mean	Standard deviation	Minimum	Maximum	Range	Median
Recognised	Minimum fee	40	280	270.5	50	1400	1350	200
	Maximum fee	40	434	366.0	50	1800	1750	350
Unrecognised	Minimum fee	945	161	143.9	20	2500	2480	150
	Maximum fee	945	240	211.3	30	3000	2970	200
NOC	Minimum fee	4	419	286.8	125	800	675	375
	Maximum fee	4	600	255.0	250	850	600	650
Total	Minimum fee	989	167	154.0	20	2500	2480	150
	Maximum fee	989	249	223.9	30	3000	2970	200

Source: Rangaraju et al. (2012).

uniform for girls, midday meal and free text books) '95% of parents stated that their preferred school type was LFP' – low-fee private.[35] However, even though fees are low, there will be some who cannot afford to send their children to low-cost private schools.[36] Half of the parents interviewed in J.P. Nagar, UP, indicated they could not afford the low fees payable in the low-cost private schools, but 95 per cent of parents said they desired private education for their children rather than government schools.

PUPIL ATTAINMENT IN PUBLIC AND PRIVATE SCHOOLS

It is often assumed that low-cost private schools are of a lower quality than government schools. However the research highlighted above shows that in the majority of cases low-cost private schools are offering a superior learning environment where teachers are more likely to be teaching when they should be and the facilities are comparable or better in both recognised and unrecognised schools than government ones.

But the argument still persists that teachers in low-cost private schools are not as well qualified, are paid significantly less and are not teacher trained compared to government schoolteachers. It is therefore assumed they cannot be providing an education to the children comparable to government schools. Monazza Aslam and Geeta Kingdon investigated teacher characteristics and practices that mattered to student achievement in government and private schools in the Punjab in Pakistan. They found that teacher certification and training, so important to those who believe government schoolteachers to be more effective 'has no bearing on pupil's standardised achievement'.[37] What are found to be significant in improving student outcomes are process variables such as teachers who plan lessons or who ask questions of pupils during lessons:

> it is often un-captured teaching 'process' variables that impact student achievement – lesson planning, involving students through asking questions during class and quizzing them on past material all substantially benefit pupil learning.[38]

It was also found that 'higher teacher pay is not associated with improvements in students' test scores'.[39] Teacher pay in both India and Pakistan is often inflated by strong teacher unions and by recruitment that is highly politicised rather than being merit based. Government teaching positions are often permanent and lack accountability. Teacher training for government teachers is 'poor when available, extremely dated with little innovation, and has little relation to teaching the teacher how to teach once in school'.[40]

In Delhi, Yuki Ohara found that parents who send their children to low-cost private unrecognised schools in Shahdara believe that teacher commitment defines a 'good teacher':

> almost all of the parents who were interviewed perceive commitment as more important than qualifications ... some parents referred to local government school teachers when explaining why commitment is more important than qualifications. These parents claimed that, although government teachers are qualified, they do not teach.[41]

Indeed, considering data from 20 Indian states and the better performance of private schools then 'we see that combining the effects of a lower pupil teacher ratio and a higher level of teaching activity leads to a child in the private school having 3–4 times more teacher contact time than in the public school'.[42]

The politicisation of the government teaching profession has been linked to the poor performance of public education in India,[43] where teacher union activities are supported by professional teacher politicians and are having a deleterious effect on student outcomes. According to Kingdon and Muzammil, in UP, government schoolteachers 'have guaranteed representation in the upper house of the state legislature' and PA teachers (private managed schools whose teachers receive salary payments from the government and thus receive grant in aid) are able to 'contest elections to the lower house because they are deemed to hold an "office of profit" under the government'. Therefore government teachers have 'substantial representation' in parliament. 'In addition, the district-level chiefs of many prominent political parties are from the teaching community'.[44] Teachers who have held a post for three years in a secondary school are able to elect one-twelfth of the members of the State Legislative Council, according to the Constitution of India Article 171 (3c). Teachers, as part of a limited number of groups, are able to elect Members of the Legislative Council (MLC). In UP, in 2004 for example, around one-quarter of UP Legislative Council members were teachers or ex-teachers.

Interestingly, teacher unions have been seen to campaign over the years 'almost invariably' on teacher pay and job security (in which they have been considerably successful)[45] 'and rarely, if ever, for broader improvements in the schooling system or for the promotion of education in general'.[46] Looking at GOI figures in the government sector, 97 per cent of primary education expenditure by 1981 was on teacher salaries, the remaining 3 per cent being the total available for non-teacher expenses. The figures for teacher salaries for junior and secondary government schooling were 94 per cent and 90 per cent respectively, leaving only 6 per cent and 10 per cent for non-salary school expenses. In 1985 the GOI said:

> more than 90% of the expenditure – in some states even more than 98% – is spent on teachers' salaries and administration. Practically nothing is available to buy a blackboard and chalks, let alone charts, other inexpensive teaching aids or even pitchers for drinking water.[47]

Teaching activity in government schools is sometimes lost owing to teachers participating in union and political activities. Protest action implies loss of teaching hours, but also teachers who are members of the Legislative Assemblies or the Legislative Councils retain their posts as government teachers; fulfilling both duties is difficult, however no replacement teachers are employed.

Drawing two salaries, one from teaching and the other from being a full-time union leader or a teacher Member of Legislative Assembly (MLA) or MLC is typical, even though teachers do not teach during this full-term in political office.[48] Research has shown that teachers who belong to a teacher union (all be it in higher cost private schools in India) had a negative effect on student outcomes. Students who were taught a subject by a unionised teacher scored around a quarter of a standard deviation lower in that subject than in others taught by a non-unionised teacher, even though unionised teachers received 'substantially higher pay'.[49]

With regard to learning levels, according to Pratham and the ASER 2011 report on rural India, in 2011 things were not looking very good. Reading levels were declining in states across North India. The proportion of children in grade five who were able to read a grade two text had dropped from 53.7 per cent in 2010 to 48.2 per cent in 2011. However, in southern states the decline was not so visible. In Gujarat, Punjab and Tamil Nadu the statistics showed better results over the year. Basic math tests overall typically showed a decline. Nationally the proportion of standard three children able to solve a two-digit subtraction using borrowing dropped from 36.3 per cent in 2010 to 29.9 per cent in 2011. In other words, fewer than one-third of children around the age of eight years could carry out a basic subtraction problem and get it correct. This was so in almost every state. The National Council of Educational Research and Training (NCERT) concurred. Testing grade three students in basic literacy showed that around one in five students nationally failed, one in three failed a basic math test.[50] In Chhattisgarh, almost all students failed both math and reading tests. A survey in Uttar Pradesh and Madhya Pradesh found that the majority of fourth and fifth grade students failed multiple choice questions in math and literacy designed for fourth graders.[51]

From an international standpoint some research has shown that India has fallen behind other countries. In one study, grade nine students from Orissa and Rajasthan in all school management types and in both rural and urban areas were given math questions from the Trends in International Mathematics and Science Study (TIMSS). The Indian students performed poorly, ranking towards the bottom in a sample of 51 countries.[52] The results show that children are falling behind in both Orissa and Rajasthan:

> The median enrolled child in these two states is a failing child, in that 42% of enrolled children in Rajasthan and 50% in Orissa fail to meet a basic international low benchmark of mathematical knowledge. Children enrolled in secondary schools in these two Indian states are 3.1 (OECD) standard deviations below the OECD mean.[53]

Looking at individual math questions it was found that the grade nine students were not able to master content categories expected for their age, such as fractions, geometry, algebra, measurement and data representation. For example, only 11 per cent of children in Rajasthan and 17 per cent in Orissa could rightly select the smallest number from a set of five decimals. Only one-third in each of the states could divide fractions. The two Indian states are 0.7 standard deviations below the TIMSS mean and 3.1 standard deviations below the OECD (Organisation for Economic Co-operation and Development) mean. However, there is great inequality in the distribution of the children's scores. One per cent of children in the states pass the advanced benchmark set by TIMSS and are able to compute, organise, solve, apply and interpret mathematical information and problems. In contrast, 42 per cent in Rajasthan and 50 per cent in Orissa pass the lowest benchmark, implying only some very basic mathematical knowledge. The data show that the most significant explanation of test score variation is the school, 32 per cent for Orissa and 41 per cent for Rajasthan.

Testing of children in various subjects, including math, English and home language, has been undertaken in developing countries around the world, including India. Data have also been gathered on pupils' family background, innate ability, school and teacher characteristics in order to control not only for school choice and therefore selection bias, but to take into account peer influences and other variables that might affect achievement. Various analytical techniques have been used to analyse the data, including multilevel modelling and the Heckman–Lee procedure. Typically the results show that pupils in low-cost private schools outperform those in government schools, and at a fraction of the teacher cost.[54]

In Hyderabad, analysing data using multilevel modelling from 3910 pupils attending government, private recognised and unrecognised schools shows that pupils in both types of private schools, after controlling for age, pupils' IQ (intelligence quotient) and class average IQ, achieve higher scores in math and English than pupils in government schools.[55] In Delhi, using a multitude of econometric techniques including the Heckman–Lee procedure, data from 3495 students from the three school types show private pupils positively and significantly outperform government pupils in math, English and Hindi.[56]

In rural India pupils in private schools significantly outperform government pupils:

> [T]here is consistent evidence of a private schooling advantage throughout the methodologies ... and after controlling for age and gender, private school attendees have cognitive achievement between 0.20 and 0.25 standard deviations (SD) higher than government school attendees. This is about seven times the effect of gender, and almost equal to the effect of an extra year of education, on average over the age range 6–14.[57]

In Orissa, India, Sangeeta Goyal found the private school effect to be positive and statistically significant in math and reading.[58] With 1859 government school pupils and 548 private school pupils taking reading and math tests and controlling for background variables as well as selection bias[59] the private school effect is large on test scores. For reading comprehension, the average private school effect after controlling for selection bias, background and other inputs is 15.4 percentage points. For math the adjusted average private school effect for grade four is 16 percentage points.

And in private low-cost schools operating in the villages of the Sehore District of Madhya Pradesh, children were being admitted and were passing Class X board exams:

> We can infer that the private schools in our study were clearly outperforming the government schools primarily in terms of offering instruction outside of the government curriculum and preparing children for the major board exams.[60]

In an all India survey carried out in 20 states, focusing on rural areas, not only did private schools have lower teacher absenteeism and higher teaching activity, but pupils scored significantly higher in tests given. After controlling for family background and other characteristics, the private school effect is still strongly significant and 'of considerable magnitude (0.4 standard deviations on the test)'.[61]

Studies from Pakistan, mainly stemming from the 'Learning and Educational Achievement in Pakistan Schools' (LEAPS) project, have shown that private schools outperform government ones.[62] In Pakistan, children from public schools perform 0.8 to 1.0 standard deviations lower on independently administered tests than do 'equivalent children in private schools'.[63] Children attending government schools in Pakistan would need 1.5–2.5 years to catch up with children in low-cost private schools.[64] Third grade children in government and private schools were tested in Urdu, math and English for the LEAPS project in 828 schools in 112 villages in three districts of the Punjab. In total, over 12,000 students took the test and of these 6241 provided data on child characteristics. The findings show that children in the third grade in Pakistan 'can barely read and write or perform the simplest arithmetic operations such as counting and addition'.[65] The differences in children's outcomes attributed to children coming from different parental backgrounds, that is poor and non-poor households, are 'dwarfed' by those attributed to attending a private or a government school. The results show that the difference in English test scores between government and private schools is 12 times the gap between those of rich and poor families. For math the difference in scores between government and private schools is eight times the gap between children with literate and illiterate fathers. Finally, for Urdu the difference between government and private schools is 18 times the difference for children with literate and illiterate mothers.

Figure 3.1 shows the unadjusted and adjusted gaps for math, English and Urdu for children attending private and government schools. The gaps are presented through a knowledge scale.

The worst child scores 0, the best 1000 and the average 500. The standard deviation for the distribution is 150. Therefore a child who scores 650 is one standard deviation above the average, one who scores 350 is one standard deviation below the mean. The largest knowledge gap is for English, where private schools outperform government ones by almost 149 knowledge points on the unadjusted score, which is one standard deviation above. For math the gap is 76 points and Urdu 101 points. The adjusted score shows the gap after controlling for family wealth, mother and father literacy rates, the child's age and gender and village fixed effects. Even after these controls, the gap hardly decreases.

The most striking gaps arise not between children but between schools in the same village. Private schools score significantly higher than government schools, even after controlling for characteristics of the student population. But there are large variations within government schools. Even in villages with a great number of poorly performing schools there is usually one school that performs well. While the best schools are not always private schools, the worst schools are almost exclusively government schools. These dismally performing government schools often record achievement levels so low that the pupils tested must have virtually no cumulated knowledge or skills after four years of education.[66]

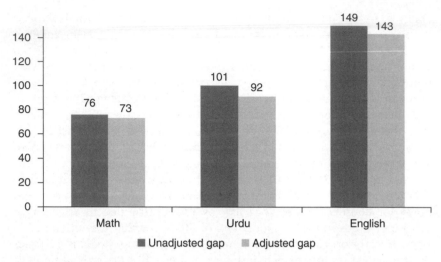

Source: Das et al. (2006), p. 40 – Leaps Exam, 2004. The mean difference between
children in private and government schools.

*Figure 3.1   Adjusted and unadjusted knowledge score gaps for private and
government schools in Pakistan*

Table 3.14 shows the percentage of children that answered specific questions correctly in the LEAPS test by school type. In every question a higher proportion of children in private schools knew the answer.

To summarise, the findings from rural Pakistan show that:

- 50 per cent of the total variation in test scores can be attributed to the school type the child attends;
- in all subjects the best schools are private with the median private school being equivalent to the top fifth percentile of government schools;
- the worst performing schools are always government in all three subjects and by a large margin;
- the range of variation between private schools (the top and worst performing) is less than the variation in government schools.

There are also beneficial consequences in communities where private schools exist. For example, in the settlements of Pakistan where a private school exists, male and female enrollments increase by 21 and 29 percentage points respectively compared to settlements without a private school.[67]

Table 3.14 Individual questions and correct answers by school type in Pakistan

Subject	The question	Percentage who answered correctly			Standard
		All	Govt	Private	
Mathematics	4 + 6	89	87	92	K & I
Mathematics	36 + 61	86	84	90	K & I
Mathematics	8 − 3	65	63	71	K & I
Mathematics	5 × 4	59	55	67	II
Mathematics	238 − 129	32	29	39	II
Mathematics	384 ÷ 6	19	17	24	III
Mathematics	4 × 32	50	46	59	III
English	Write the letter 'D' (spoken out loud)	86	82	93	
English	Fill in the right letter D _ F	70	62	87	
English	Fill in the missing letters (picture of a ball) BA _ _	45	35	69	
English	Fill in the missing letters (picture of a flag) F L A _	29	20	48	
Urdu	Write a sentence with the word "beautiful"	33	27	49	
Urdu	Write a sentence with the word "school"	31	24	46	

Source: Questions are from the Pakistan LEAPS exam, Das et al. (2006), p. 36.

Monazza Aslam tested 1887 grade eight children in numeracy and math from a total of 65 schools (25 government and 40 private) in rural and urban Lahore. Data were also collected on pupil and family characteristics and a test for IQ was also administered. The findings again show a substantial private school achievement advantage, even controlling for background and individual characteristics equal to about 0.35 standard deviations of the achievement score.[68] Again, as in the LEAPS project, around 46 per cent of the achievement advantage of private school pupils over government school pupils can be attributed to school effects. Private school advantage is 'substantial'.[69]

Very few studies have been carried out to investigate what happens to children from low-income areas after they have left private and state schools. The whole research area is still in its infancy and very few longitudinal studies have been possible to date. This is something that aid money could focus on.

One piece of research that has been carried out by Mohammad Asadullah has looked at the wage rates graduates from both private and state schools in Bangladesh and Pakistan can expect. Interestingly, in Bangladesh many of the secondary schools are PA, whereas in Pakistan aided schools are non-existent.[70] The findings indicate that in Pakistan a wage premium is enjoyed by those educated in private schools over their government schooled peers. In Bangladesh there seems to be no advantage, which could be attributed to the private schools' aided status:

> private aided schools which have mushroomed over the past years in Bangladesh under guaranteed government finance, without any link between grant money and student achievement. Teachers and managers of aided schools today have little incentive to perform. As teachers of public and aided schools are paid on same salary scale, the same incentive problem plagues public schools so that aided and public schools have possibly become indistinguishable.[71]

By contrast, findings from Pakistan show that PUA school graduates do possess superior individual characteristics over government school graduates. However, over and above these the private school effect on wages is positive and substantial, accounting for about 43 per cent of the total wage premium. Some of the higher returns are determined because of the superior language skills ability gained by private school students, possibly by being educated in English.

CONCLUSIONS AND DISCUSSION

It is acknowledged that a low-cost private education sector is serving low-income families in developing countries. In part, it is suggested that this sector has emerged because of the low quality of available government schools. However, there are also doubts raised about the relative quality of this private provision, particularly that not approved by government, but from the data these worries seem unfounded. It is hoped that this chapter, reporting on studies from around India exploring the nature and extent of private schools and comparing inputs across school management types, can help improve our understanding of the phenomenon.

Research shows that private schools are more cost-effective with better learning outcomes where salaries for teachers reflect the market rate value of their services and not an inflated salary owing to union or political pressure. Private schools in general show a lower level of teacher absence and in all cases a higher level of activity in the classroom. The pupil–teacher ratio in private schools is smaller and operating on commercial principles implies accountability to parents who are fee-paying and able to choose another school if dissatisfied with their current one. By contrast, government schoolteachers are guaranteed a job for life and are rewarded on the basis of years of service not performance. Parents, recognising that government schools are failing and not offering them the kind of education they require for their children, have voted with their feet to the PUA schools in both rural and urban areas.

Studies suggest that the private sector is certainly a significant provider. However, there are two major concerns about the role of PUA schools in general, and unrecognised private schools in particular, which the research findings here may usefully illuminate.

First, private schools charge fees, thus making them out of reach of the poorest.[72] But *per se* this might not be an insurmountable obstacle for PUA schools assisting in meeting 'education for all' goals: PUA schools themselves engage in offering informal scholarships (free or concessionary places) for some of the poorest children to attend.[73] One approach would be to extend this principle to create state and/or donor-funded targeted vouchers for the poorest, or for girls (hence potentially overcoming any gender disparity in enrolment that is suggested), to use at private schools, which could overcome this objection. This option will be discussed further in the Chapter 4. UNDP accepts this as a possible way forward:

> To ensure that children from poor families unable to pay school fees are able to attend private schools, governments could finance their education through vouchers.[74]

It notes the success of two targeted voucher programmes, in Colombia and Pakistan, the latter targeted at girls. There would seem to be no *a priori* reasons why such programmes could not be introduced into the Indian context, which would overcome this first objection to private schools as a vehicle for education for all. Interestingly, the Probe Report revealed an overwhelming majority of rural poor parents would prefer to send their children to private schools, if they had the funds.[75] Targeted vouchers would be one way of enhancing these parental desires, if they were also found in the populations studied. This is one option that will be looked at in more detail in Chapter 4.

Moreover, it appears from the discussion above that providing such vouchers might be a cost-effective way of increasing enrolment of the poorest. For mean monthly teacher salaries and per pupil teacher salaries are considerably lower in PUA (recognised and unrecognised) than government schools – and teacher salaries are likely to make up the vast majority of recurrent expenditure in schools (in India, estimated to be 93 per cent of all recurrent expenditure in government primary schools).[76] Extending access to the poorest through targeted vouchers for PUA schools may be a less expensive option than increasing enrolment in government schools. If one of the reasons for lower private school enrolment in rural than urban areas is because fewer parents are able to afford fees, then such targeted vouchers may also lead to an increase in the supply side of such schools in rural areas, just as their numbers have increased in urban areas where fee-paying capacity is higher, although further research may be required to explore exactly how the market would respond.

However, the second concern is of the quality of provision in private schools serving the poor, particularly unrecognised ones – implying that extending access to such schools would not be desirable because of the low quality of education within them. The research findings offer some insights here. Considering the quality indicators investigated in the surveys, comparing government and unrecognised PUA schools, private schools perform well, with great teacher activity and often facilities that are comparable to or better than government school facilities. These conclusions suggest that any concerns about extending access to unrecognised PUA schools on the grounds of their low quality may be somewhat misplaced, for they are currently in general offering better or as good quality (at least according to these inputs) than government schools. No one appears to be suggesting that because government schools are of low quality access should not be extended to them, instead ways are explored of improving their quality. The same consideration would seem to be possible concerning unrecognised private schools.

One way forward noted by many commentators is to bring unrecognised private schools under state regulations, to ensure that quality is improved. For some researchers note that recognition in India does not necessarily signify meeting regulations, but often 'unofficial payments' or bribes paid to inspectors. This suggests that the impetus for school improvement may not come (or not only) from a desire to be recognised by government, but from other factors, such as meeting parental demand. Further research is needed to uncover exactly what the factors are that lead to the more superior inputs in recognised than unrecognised private schools. One hypothesis worth exploring, supported by these observations, is that private schools are able to seek recognition as they become more mature, attracting more students and raising their fees, so that they are able to invest more in school improvement, and pay the costs of recognition. The smaller class sizes, by this hypothesis, in the unrecognised private schools may simply be a result of having *vacancies* in a classroom, rather than a deliberate policy, an advantage that would vanish if the unrecognised schools became larger over time (although recognised private schools have smaller class sizes than PA and government schools, so would still offer this advantage to parents and children).

Whatever such research might uncover, the conclusion of this chapter is that apprehensions expressed about the 'mushrooming' of PUA schools serving the poor, including unrecognised ones, may not be powerful objections to exploring ways in which such schools might become part of the solution to providing 'education for all', rather than be seen as a cause for concern. What is more is that the Right to Education Act (2010) (RTE) implies that all unrecognised schools that remain with an 'unrecognised' status in 2013 will be closed down. The research highlighted here shows that would be a big mistake. Not only a costly one, but one based on prejudices as unrecognised schools typically outperform, with regard achievement and facilities, government ones at a fraction of the teacher cost. Were these schools closed down places would have to be found for a good proportion of children who live in slum and low-income areas. Where would they find places? And at what cost to the government of India? So, how to deal with unrecognised PUA schools if the aim is for them to gain recognition status, which they cannot achieve as the rules and regulations are too stringent and costly, and typically do not target quality? The answer could lie in a regulatory regime removed from government control – that is either self-regulation or private accreditation companies. These issues will be explored and discussed in Chapter 4. Closing down schools that are not costing the government money and that are performing better than the alternative for these children would be educational suicide. So what can the Indian government, international governments and aid agencies focus on in order to ensure that children in India, and other developing countries, have quality schooling that they are able to access and choose? Chapter 4 makes some suggestions, looking at research evidence, providing a possible recipe for the focus of international aid that could be effective and efficient.

NOTES

1. Watkins (2000), pp. 229–30.
2. Venkatanarayana (2004), p. 40.
3. The Probe Team (1999), p. 103.
4. De et al. (2002), p. 148.
5. Nambissan (2003), p. 52.
6. Aggarwal (2000), p. 20.
7. Alderman et al. (1996), p. 10.
8. World Bank (1997).
9. Andrabi et al. (2007), p. vi.
10. Aggarwal (2000), p. 21.
11. Nambissan (2003); De et al. (2002).
12. Azam et al. (2010).
13. See for example Goyal and Pandey (2009).
14. Rana et al. (2002), pp. 64 and 67.
15. Ibid., n. 28.
16. UNDP (2003), p. 112.
17. Kremer et al. (2004a), pp. 5 and 9.
18. World Bank (2003), p. 24.
19. Nambissan (2003), p. 20.
20. Mehrotra and Panchamukhi (2006), pp. 438–9.
21. Watkins (2000), p. 230.
22. Nambissan (2003), p. 52.
23. Watkins (2000), p. 230; UNDP (2003), p. 115.
24. De et al. (2011), p. 39.
25. Muralidharan and Kremer (2008).
26. Census of India (2001).
27. See Mehta (2002).
28. Pratham (2011).
29. See for example Kingdon (1996).
30. De et al. (2002); and Nambissan (2003), for example.
31. Pratham (2012).
32. Härmä (2009), p. 158.
33. See Goyal and Pandey (2009).
34. Government of India (2005), 2001 figures.
35. Härmä (2009), p. 158.
36. Härmä (2009).
37. Aslam and Kingdon (2007), p. 12.
38. Ibid., p. 14.
39. Ibid., p. 15.
40. Ibid., p. 17; see also Kingdon and Teal (2010).
41. Ohara (2012), p. 83.
42. Muralidharan and Kremer (2008), p. 102.
43. Kingdon and Muzammil (2009).
44. Ibid., p. 124.

45. NCT (1986), p. 73.
46. Kingdon and Muzammil (2009), p. 135.
47. Government of India (1985), p. 25.
48. Kingdon and Muzammil (2009), p. 142.
49. Kingdon and Teal (2010), p. 284.
50. NCERT (2009).
51. Goyal and Pandey (2009).
52. Goyal (2009); and Das and Zajonc (2010).
53. Das and Zajonc (2010), p. 176.
54. Tooley et al. (2011); Tooley et al. (2010); French and Kingdon (2010); Pratham (2011); Andrabi et al. (2010); Andrabi et al. (2007).
55. Tooley et al. (2010).
56. Tooley et al. (2011).
57. French and Kingdon (2010), pp. 21 and 27.
58. Goyal (2009).
59. Ibid., using a method suggested by Altonji et al. (2005).
60. Johnson and Bowles (2010), p. 499.
61. Muralidharan and Kremer (2008), p. 105.
62. See for example Arif and Saqib (2003); Das et al. (2006); and Aslam (2007).
63. Andrabi et al. (2010).
64. Andrabi et al. (2007), pp. xiv–xv.
65. Das et al. (2006), p. 23.
66. Ibid.
67. Andrabi et al. (2008), p. 340.
68. Aslam (2009), p. 345.
69. Ibid., p. 349.
70. Asadullah (2009).
71. Ibid., p. 85.
72. Watkins (2000), p. 207; The Probe Team (1999), p. 105; UNDP (2003), p. 115.
73. Tooley and Dixon (2005).
74. UNDP (2003), p. 115.
75. The Probe Team (1999), p. 102.
76. Keefer and Khemani (2004).

A boy outside a private school in Hyderabad

Tuni orphanage
Photo by James Tullock

Tuni orphanage
Photo by James Tullock

Gateway to the Old City in Hyderabad

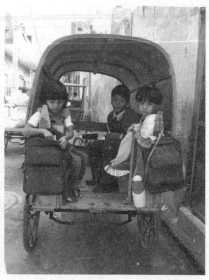

Girls with bags at a low-cost private school in Hyderabad

Cycle rickshaw taking children to and from a private school in Delhi

Tuni orphanage girls
Photo by James Tullock

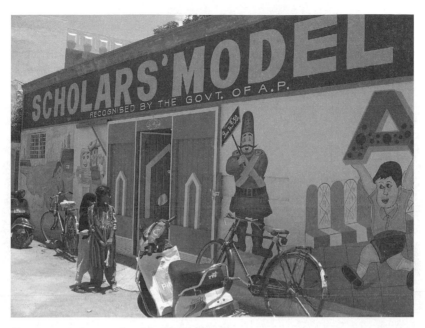

Low-cost private school in Hyderabad

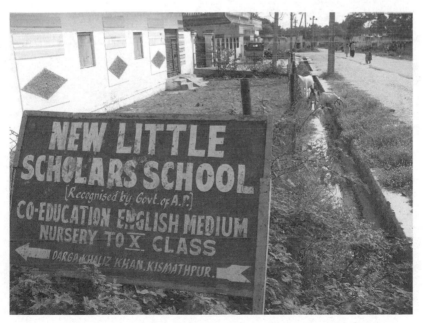

Low-cost private school sign board in Andhra Pradesh

A cowshed next to a low-cost private school in Hyderabad

Mr Parvees's school in Hyderabad

Boys going to school in rural AP

Peer teaching in ARK phonics ASPIRE programme, Delhi

Tuni orphanage boys
Photo by Phil Barnes

Boy at Tuni orphanage
Photo by Phil Barnes

Girls at Tuni
Photo by Phil Barnes

4 The anteroom of eternity? Gaining attention from aid agencies

So information about low-cost private schools in India has now reached the ears and eyes of the aid agencies, philanthropists and investors around the world. Chapter 3 provided a summary of current research data from different states in India, illustrating the extent of PUA school provision. These schools have been outperforming government ones at a fraction of the teacher cost. But now their heads have been raised above the parapet is this a good thing?

A general theme throughout the book has been that the state has become more involved in schooling when one could question whether it in fact needed or even intended too. Chapter 1 showed that in both India and England in the nineteenth century there were burgeoning private sectors made up of multiple suppliers of education. Children were being educated without the input of the state. However, owing to the need and desire of governments to control what was being taught the state began to encroach on all that was good, in fact destroying and crowding out in both countries the indigenous schools that initially were imparting quite successfully the ability to read, along with other subjects.

Chapter 2 once again highlights how governments and aid agencies on an international scale have thrown money at a schooling system that was put in place by the British in India. A system that now has been shown to be crumbling owing in part to the lack of accountability of government schoolteachers and strong teacher unions. A malaise and lethargy has set in within government schoolteacher ranks leading to absenteeism, a lack of activity and a belief that children from poor families are incapable of learning. The evidence of this is set out in Chapter 3. Providing aid in such circumstances is going to make little difference to student outcomes. Irrespective of the amount of money piled in to improve facilities or provide educational materials, no teaching implies no learning.

International aid agencies have now been looking at the research evidence on low-cost private schools. Aid agencies, such as DfID, are now more interested in getting a bang for their buck, and showing the taxpayer that their interventions are making a difference for the poor. The electorate are going to need some persuading if governments are going to be committing 0.7 per cent of GNI to development assistance, especially when there are multiple examples of waste, corruption and theft along with the ineffective targeting of aid.

Using a relatively new concept in focusing aid called 'making markets work for the poor' (M4P) is one way that money could actually be shown to have a positive effect on low-cost private schools and the market in which they operate.

Until very recently, it has typically been assumed that schooling is a public good, should be provided by the state and therefore is not relevant for inclusion in such schemes as the M4P, as discussed in Chapter 2. The main aim has been to fix state schooling. And with regard to some agencies, such as UNESCO and Oxfam, this is still the case.

However, M4P is an approach where donors such as DfID, SIDA and SDC (Swiss Agency for Development and Cooperation) are trying to make markets work more effectively for the poor; poverty reduction is therefore targeted by focusing on market systems in which the poor are participating.[1] Improving the market system, allowing it to work more effectively and sustainably, thus will improve the livelihoods of the poor and in turn reduce poverty. Sustainable development it is now believed can come from market-based approaches. There are several programmes from aid agencies with this focus, including:

- M4P from DfID/SIDA/SDC;
- Growing Inclusive Markets from UNDP;
- Opportunities for the Majority from IADB (Inter American Development Bank); and
- The IFC's Next Four Billion.

Engaging with those at the bottom of the pyramid to ensure sustainable development is now becoming the focus for governments, aid agencies and businesses alike. David Ferrand et al. believe that:

> Markets offer the primary means through which poor people can participate in economic activity. They can do so as producers (farmers, business owners), as employees (i.e., providers of labour) and as consumers (of goods and services). Markets operating in an inclusive manner serve the poor by offering them the things they need – jobs, opportunities, finance, products – to increase their incomes.[2]

And why is an M4P approach more likely to succeed than those before it? There are two distinctive differences. First, the objective and approach have been developed by looking at and learning from real world experiences, both successful and unsuccessful. Second, the overall methodology

can provide a framework in order to pursue specific solutions to an individual country's problems. 'It is a framework providing a shared basis
for productive debate and action. Far from being an imposed "model", it
allows countries to "reclaim" their own development'.[3]

The low-cost private schools market is perfect for M4P. Getting to the
bottom of the pyramid, increasing the ability of the poorest to participate
in the market, whilst making it more efficient at transferring knowledge
to all participants is surely a step up from throwing money at government
schools, through programmes unable to fix the unfixable as shown in the
previous chapters.

Therefore, by concentrating on markets and aiming at the grass roots
there are different interventions that agencies can bring to the low-cost
private schools' sector that could make a difference to children's access
and quality of learning. Some are investigated more fully in this chapter.
All of these interventions and ideas have been identified during research
as initiatives suggested by the school entrepreneurs, parents, teachers and
other actors within the market. That is, these ideas have been perpetuated
by Searchers participating in the low-cost schools' market, not Planners:

- Providing funding for those who currently cannot access low-cost
  private schools but want to – that is, providing choice for the
  poorest though scholarships, targeted vouchers and conditional
  (or unconditional) cash transfers, thus building on private school
  philanthropy.
- Loan schemes – school owners are hungry for investment capital,
  so funding through different initiatives such as microfinance or chit
  funds would help improve school facilities and thus quality and
  effectiveness.
- Innovation – pedagogy and curriculum development within the low-
  cost private schools' sector perpetuated by competition.
- Regulation change or private evaluation of schools – adapting the
  regulations private schools have to abide by and gain recognition in
  order to focus on those inputs that improve quality and student outcomes. This would include trying to deal with the issue of corruption
  and bribery within the system, therefore suggesting the evaluation
  process to be undertaken by private companies.
- Investments – nurturing and supporting an initial setting up of education brands and chains of low-cost private schools.
- Advocacy – capacity building, training and development for private
  school federations in order that they carry on self-sustaining
  improvements taking the market forward, as well as liaising with
  government and policy-makers.

- Issuing of property rights where possible for schools to operate legally.
- The identification and nurturing of high-ability students.

Each of these interventions is considered in this chapter. If there is to be a chance of improving the lives of the poorest then inputs need to be delivered at the grass-roots level. However, as Riddell warns, currently aid agencies have little experience of working directly with the poor, and even NGOs who typically work with small numbers of people have difficulty knowing how to scale up and extend small-scale projects.[4] Be warned. The private schools market is currently operating well but it could do with some help. However, aid agencies must not interfere with the general operation or functioning of the market. Therefore, the following suggestions minimise any possible negative effects by focusing on access and quality interventions that can be maximised and made sustainable by the market itself.

SCHOOL VOUCHERS

An education voucher may be a coupon or a cheque that a government, aid agency or philanthropist provides to parents for them to spend with an education provider of their choice. Education vouchers may be used as part or whole payment. The school may be in the state or private sector but typically it would be an approved school participating in the voucher programme. Providing money or vouchers directly to the poor minimises corruption and theft. Missing out government bureaucratic interference and involvement can only be good for progress.

The two main types of voucher programmes in education are targeted and universal vouchers. In a universal voucher scheme, all students receive a voucher for a specified value; the voucher is redeemable by the school. When there are no government subsidies, the schools are competing for students and their vouchers. The schools that stimulate student outcomes and are perceived by parents to be 'good' schools will prosper, attracting students and hence their vouchers. The schools perceived by parents to be inferior and failing would not attract students and hence funding. The failing, impoverished school will either have to improve or close.

As the name suggests targeted vouchers stimulate the same competition between schools for students, but they are only available to those who meet certain financial, educational or geographic criteria and hence are targeted.

An idea for an education voucher system was proposed over 200 years ago by Thomas Paine, who in 1791 recommended a type of targeted voucher for the poorest in the good society he was planning. In this society there would be:

> a number of families who, though not properly of the class of the poor, yet find it difficult to give education to their children ... The method will be, to allow for each of these children ten shillings a year for the expense of schooling, for six years each, which will give them six months schooling each year and half a crown for paper and spelling books.[5]

John Stuart Mill also suggested such a scheme in *On Liberty* in the mid nineteenth century, stating that the government had the right 'to require for every child a good education'; it did not need to provide or finance schooling for all:

> It might leave to parents to obtain the education where and how they pleased, and content itself with helping to pay the school fees of the poorer classes of children, and defraying the entire school expenses of those who have no-one else to pay for them.[6]

Both social reformers proposed that government funding could help the disadvantaged within society and that funding could be spent with any education provider.

Milton Friedman articulated the education voucher idea in more detail almost 60 years ago in an article published in 1955. Friedman was advocating a universal voucher that could be topped up and spent in an 'approved' educational institution of the parents' choosing. According to Friedman, governments would have a limited role of ensuring minimum standards within private institutions, which could be 'for', or 'non'-profit schools. It was a private system where parents were free to choose through the use of a voucher that Friedman believed could deliver schooling which was competitive, flexible, innovative and varied. Under a universal voucher programme costs would fall owing partly to teachers' salaries being determined by the market rather than teacher unions. Later in *Free to Choose* Milton and Rose Friedman regarded the poor state of inner-city schools in the US as a 'sickness' which could be directly attributed to 'denying many parents control over the kind of schooling their children receive either directly, through choosing and paying for the schools their children attend, or indirectly, through local political activity'.[7] Social and educational reformers wrongly assumed that poor uneducated parents have little interest in their children's education. Typically poor parents are regarded as being unable to choose the most appropriate educational establishments that best suit their needs. The Friedmans regarded this pos-tulation as a 'gratuitous insult'.[8] And rightly so, as shown by poor parents in India. Providing parents with greater control over schooling would be one way to ensure improvement in learning. In *Free to Choose*, Milton and Rose Friedman tentatively proposed a targeted voucher idea rather than a universal one.

Concerns About the Adoption of Universal Education Vouchers

Milton Friedman won the Nobel Prize in 1976 and became a member of the 'Economic Policy Advisory Board' during Ronald Reagan's presidency. Lady Thatcher was Prime Minister in the UK at this time. Both Reagan and Thatcher were inspired by Friedman's economic ideas and hence the UK government in the 1980s seriously considered the implementation of a universal education voucher programme. Friedman had already identified several concerns that dissidents of such a scheme would propose. The Thatcher government in the 1980s approached academics, including Friedman, in order for them to answer uncertainties they were having about the possible implementation and introduction of a universal voucher scheme for education in England. Fourteen academics replied to the Department of Education's fears in 1981. However it was not until October 1983, at the Conservative Party Conference, that the academics gained their response from the then Secretary of State who announced that the issue of the voucher was 'dead'.[9] So what were these concerns and why was the idea 'killed off' by politicians known for their forwardness and keenness to implement new policies?

Friedman had already identified several concerns regarding the adoption of a universal education voucher programme. These concerns again were reiterated during the consultation in the 1980s between the Thatcher government and academics.

- increased cost to taxpayers;
- inelastic supply of schools;
- parental inability to choose;
- negative impact on state schools and the state sector;
- education law and acts would need to change in order to allow a voucher scheme to operate;
- fraud.

These concerns will be raised again and tackled when considering the possible funding of a targeted voucher programme for India though aid money.

The Evidence

There are now a large number of successful voucher schemes not only in the US, but also in Sweden, Chile, Colombia, Pakistan and India.

The Columbia voucher scheme illustrates a successful implementation of education vouchers, which is raising education standards among the poor. It has proved so successful that governments and social entrepreneurs internationally are being encouraged to consider implementing such a scheme. The targeted voucher scheme, the Programa de Ampliación de Cobertura de la Educación Secundaria (PACES), was set up just over 20 years ago and provided vouchers to help 125,000 children from low-income families. The voucher covers just over half of the average cost of private secondary schooling. Those initially targeted were low-income families with children about to start secondary school who were living in areas classified in the two lowest socio-economic strata. As proof of residency, families had to provide a utility bill to apply and illustrate their eligibility. Parents could only send their children to participating schools. In 1996 for-profit private schools were excluded from parental choice. Vouchers were issued continuously until the end of the 11th grade, the final year of secondary school, as long as the child progressed through each grade successfully.

Researchers have tracked these children over the years. They also tracked a similar number of families who had applied for but were not allocated vouchers, due to limited numbers, through a randomised control trial (RCT).

The results show that not only did parents who were given vouchers opt to send their children to private schools – and not keep them in the state system – but that the children stayed on until eighth grade (about 13 years old), were less likely to take paid work during school time – therefore concentrate on their studies – and they scored higher in achievement tests than their peers who attended government schools. The number of youngsters graduating from high school rose by 5–7 per cent. And they were also more likely to try for university.[10]

The Chilean voucher scheme that started in 1981 has been researched extensively. Some find positive effects on test scores[11] and others no impact on test scores or enrolment.[12] This could be because of the lack of random assignment and the inability to determine whether variation in school choice is endogenous.[13] However, what can be said is that the reforms saw the expansion of secondary schooling resulting from private school participation; this led to an increase in student participation in secondary schools and a decrease in drop-out rates at the very least.

The Punjab Education Foundation (PEF) has been running the Education Voucher Scheme (EVS) in Lahore since 2006. In 2011 a total of

40,000 vouchers were offered in 17 districts, including Lahore, at a value of PRs. 350 ($3.71) per child, per month. A yearly payment of PRs. 1000 ($10.57) is also given to parents to buy books, stationery and uniforms. Over half of the voucher recipients are girls. The aim of the scheme is to allow the 'poorest of the poor' to 'have equal access to quality education'.[14] Private schools apply to be included in the programme and parents can only choose to spend their vouchers in EVS partner schools. If fees are more than the voucher amount, schools are not allowed to ask parents to top up. Partner schools are not only accountable to the parents who are spending their vouchers with them but also to PEF who carry out reviews of student learning and inspections of the facilities, and monitor any updating through investment or improvements that the schools within the programme are carrying out. At least half of the students tested in a school need to score at least 40 per cent in the test provided by PEF. Schools are excluded from the programme if they fail two successive test periods. PEF carries out professional development programmes in all participating schools three times a year and provides teachers with lesson plans in order to develop teacher quality. Summer camps are provided for children who have not been to school before, providing an adjustment period when other children are not in school as well as bringing learning levels up to or near peer standards. Ninety-seven per cent of households participating in the EVS earn less than PRs. 7000 per month ($74). Breadwinners of families utilising the vouchers are typically daily wage labourers, household servants or engaged in other unskilled labour, including some who are 'hawkers' and unemployed. Children already in government schools were not allowed to apply for a voucher.

In the USA more than 190,000 students attend private schools using public funding.[15] School choice programmes in America include voucher programmes and tax credit scholarships. They are operating in 16 states as well as Washington DC. Of the ten randomised control trials examining the effects vouchers have on students, nine find a positive outcome, six of these nine show that all students benefit and three show that some benefit and others are not affected. Only one study shows no impact. No study has found a negative impact. It has been estimated that from 1990–2006 there has been a saving of $422 million for local school districts and $22 million for state budgets owing to school choice programmes.[16] When a student leaves a government school to attend a private school using a voucher, this leaves government schools with more money and resources to serve those who stay in public education.[17]

Parents have been shown to be more satisfied with schools they choose through vouchers than parents in government schools. Jay Greene's study in Charlotte finds parents using vouchers more likely to rate their school an 'A' compared to government school parents (53 per cent versus 26 per cent). They are also more likely to be very satisfied with school inputs, including being very satisfied with teaching in their school (54 per cent of parents) compared to parents in government schools (27 per cent).[18] William Howell and Paul Peterson looked at parental satisfaction in Dayton, New York and Washington with 16 variables; voucher parents stated they had much higher satisfaction on all of the variables, including the following: academic program (54 per cent versus 15 per cent), what is taught (55.5 per cent versus 15 per cent), teacher skills (58 per cent versus 18 per cent), school discipline (53 per cent versus 15 per cent), and moral values (52 per cent versus 17 per cent).[19]

Currently, a number of highly disadvantaged students in the US attend school through voucher schemes. The majority are from low-income, African American, Latino and single-parent families. The Milwaukee Parental Choice Program (MPCP) has been running since 1990 and is funded by the State of Wisconsin at an estimated cost to the taxpayer of US$6,442 per student, compared to a cost of $15,034 per student for Milwaukee public (state) schools. MPCP has 20,000 participants who are from low-income families and inclusive of grades pre-K to grade 12 (4–5 year olds to 17–18 year olds).[20]

In a wide-ranging study of ten voucher schemes, Professor Patrick Wolf from the University of Arkansas concluded that the children who benefitted most from the schemes in the US were African American students who came from poor homes and who, had it not been for the vouchers, would otherwise have had to attend a poorly performing public school.[21]

Research that has used the gold standard of randomised control trials, and there are ten such studies, show that children using vouchers outperform those who do not. The participants in the programme have been randomly assigned by a lottery to be either in the control or treatment groups. That is, students who win the lottery are offered vouchers and then compared with those who lost the lottery and are not offered vouchers. RCTs have been carried out on the following voucher programmes: Milwaukee, Charlotte, Dayton Ohio, Washington DC and New York. Table 4.1 summarises some of the findings.

In the early years, the evidence shows that for the Milwaukee programme voucher students performed higher on reading and math scores using state-collected data. Other studies have also shown positive results in math scores. Two sets of research show positive effects of the privately funded Charlotte NC programme, even after only one year of receiving the voucher. Again the privately funded Washington DC voucher programme showed voucher students to have scored 7.5 points higher than non-voucher students in a math and reading test after two years. However, owing to 71 per cent of children deciding not to use the voucher in the third year the results for the testing in that year can be dismissed. It seems that the students left the programme in order to attend free publically funded Charter schools, as the vouchers needed to be topped up and did not cover the full cost of attending a private school. The programme in Dayton shows that black students scored 6.5 points higher in a math and reading test after two years of using the voucher. And, similarly, in New York City, black students using the vouchers scored nine points higher than non-voucher pupils in a math and reading test. Some reanalysis of the New York data has been discredited owing to the utilisation of students with missing data, the exclusion of baseline scores and the reclassification of race where self-identification was missing.[22] Graduation rates were found to be improved by 12 percentage points for pupils using education vouchers – 82 per cent graduation rate compared to 70 per cent for non-voucher users.

It is often asserted that vouchers could skim the cream of children from public schools. Research shows, however, that education vouchers have a positive impact on academic achievement in government schools. Out of 19 studies carried out between 2001 and 2010, only one shows no impact and the remaining 18 show that vouchers improve government schools. The Washington DC voucher programme, which showed no visible effect of vouchers on public schools, is the only programme to provide more funding to public schools to compensate them for the loss of students through vouchers. It can be argued that public schools are therefore protected from the competition vouchers bring to public schools. Hence, in this isolated case, no visible effect.

Countries as diverse as the more social-democratic Sweden have evolved voucher schemes that provide for children from low-income backgrounds. The voucher programme in Sweden was introduced in 1992. One aim of the Swedish voucher scheme was to stimulate the opening of new schools, so that parents in poor localities had the power to choose. This saw a right for anyone to be able to start and run a school. The school receives funding matching the average per student cost, and this is paid by the municipality in which the school is situated. All of the school's funding comes from vouchers. Both for-profit and non-profit schools are permissible. Independent schools are not allowed to charge top-up fees and therefore profits can only be made by the number of voucher students the school attracts. Before 1992 less than 1 per cent of students in compulsory education attended independent schools, now that figure is about 10 per cent in total, and 20 per cent for upper secondary school students.[23]

It is generally accepted across the Swedish political spectrum that competition from independent schools benefitting from the voucher scheme

Table 4.1 Randomised control trial results on US voucher programmes

Location	Years	Published	Author	Positive effect		No visible effect	Test	
				All students	Some students		reading	math
Washington DC (public funding)	6	2010	Wolf et al.	All			Improved graduation rates by 12 percentage points	
Charlotte, NC (private)	1	2008	Cowen	All			8 points higher	7 points higher
New York (private)	3	2004	Krueger & Zhu			No visible effect	Discredited statistical model	
New York (private)	1	2003	Barnard et al.		Some			5 points higher
New York (private)	3	2002	Howell & Peterson		Some		Black students scored 9 points higher in combined test	
Washington DC (private funding)	3		Howell & Peterson	All			After 2 years 7.5 points higher in combination. After 3 years no visible effect (71% of voucher students left the programme in year 3)	
Dayton (private)	2		Howell & Peterson		Some		Black students 6.5 points higher on combined test	
Charlotte, NC	1	2001	Greene	All			Combined 6 points higher	
Milwaukee (public)	4	1998	Greene et al.	All			6 points higher	11 points higher
Milwaukee (public)	4	1998	Rouse	All				8 points higher

Source: Forster (2011).

has improved results and raised standards in all schools, including state schools.[24] The findings show that:

> the impact of a 10 percentage point increase in the share of independent-school students has resulted in close to a 2 percentile rank higher educational achievement at the end of compulsory school and in high school, a 2 percentage point higher probability of choosing an academic high-school track, a 2 percentage point higher probability of attending university and almost 4 weeks more schooling.[25]

These positive effects are mainly owing to the spillover or competition effects and not because independent school students are performing better than government school ones.

So the positive effects of vouchers are being felt not only in the US, but in Europe and some developing countries too. They allow greater choice for children and parents; greater accountability for the consumer; improvements of schools through competition – not only private but also government; stimulate entrepreneurship; and stimulate higher achievement outcomes. The voucher schemes should be embraced by aid agencies as they consider providing international aid to developing country education systems. Private schools for the poor are burgeoning in India and Africa, and by offering targeted vouchers the scheme provides a perfect platform to improve access and quality of education for those who are currently unable to afford it.

BACK TO INDIA

Indeed, if the voucher programme was targeted and introduced in India each of the concerns raised by Milton Friedman could be resolved. As set out above, the concerns included:

- increased cost to taxpayers;
- inelastic supply of schools;
- parental inability to choose;
- negative impact on state schools and the state sector;
- education law and acts would need to change in order to allow a voucher scheme to operate;
- fraud.

Taking each of these in turn; first, data from developing countries show that low-cost private schools are more efficient than government schools. A voucher scheme in India would be cheaper for both the taxpayer and government. Low-cost private schools are much more cost-effective than government schools owing in part to the much lower teacher salaries and lack of bureaucratic funding required. Private school provision in India is very flexible. Hundreds of thousands of low-cost private schools are already providing schooling to children in India. Vouchers would only increase the supply of schools, especially in rural areas. The supply of low-cost private schools is elastic, the greater the demand, the more low-cost private schools operate owing to the fact that they run for-profit and account for someone's livelihood. In India private schools are relatively inexpensive to set up and do not need to meet regulations, at least initially. With regard to state school quality, it could be asserted that competition from the low-cost private schools would instil in government schools the need to improve. However, what needs to accompany the private school competition element is the possibility for government schools to be closed down due to poor performance. This would then stimulate government school improvement, as shown in the voucher programmes in the US and Sweden. The existence of low-cost private schools around the world has dispelled the myth that low-income parents are incapable of making a choice. Indeed, from a historical standpoint it has been shown in Chapter 1 that prior to the state taking over education from the already flourishing indigenous education provision, parents in India were making decisions with regard to their children's education. State laws and rules with regard to schooling are still being put together in India. This would be a perfect time therefore for the education rules to be written to allow vouchers and parental choice to flourish. Finally, the issue of fraud is one that needs to be addressed. However, the size of fraud committed or that is possible while targeting those at the grass roots is likely to be much smaller and more difficult than giving money to governments for top-down intervention and implementation.

So, poor parents in India and other developing countries want choices. They want to send their children to a school of their choosing. Voucher schemes for a country like India need to be well-designed, taking into account 'regulation, support services and finance'.[26] Decisions are required concerning the rules that parents, schools and children need to adhere to. Support is required for the schools supplying voucher places and households who are availing themselves of the vouchers, typically for the first time. Finance not only implies determining what the most appropriate voucher amount should be, but also ensuring smooth monetary transactions via the submission of the voucher from the parent to the school and then back to the school entrepreneur from those funding the voucher programme. There is also the need to source the finance and define the total cost of the programme. Decisions are required with regard to location, the size of the scheme, family eligibility criteria, the system for distributing and collecting vouchers, frequency of payment, and empanelling the schools that are to participate. All schemes should be evaluated using gold standard research methods such as an RCT. There are currently two voucher schemes operating in India that are being evaluated using RCTs, one in Delhi and the other in rural Andhra Pradesh.

The Delhi voucher programme is known as ENABLE (Ensure Access to Better Learning Experiences). It is funded by a London based charity, Absolute Return for Kids (ARK), and the vouchers are being distributed to families living in the slum area in Delhi known as Shahdara. The 1618 children who applied for the vouchers were divided into two groups using a lottery. The treatment group are those who were offered vouchers and the control group those not offered vouchers. This then allowed for analysis through a randomised control trial to evaluate the programme as little is known about the effects of vouchers in India or Africa. The number of vouchers allocated was around 835 in 2011; by mid August 2012, 673 children were still using the vouchers in 68 low-cost private schools.

Initially the applicants had to provide information concerning their economic status to show they were from 'economically weaker sections', implying the parents were earning no more than Rs. 8000/- per month (around $143.24 per month), which is around one Lakh rupees per year (Rs. 100,000/-), about $1,790.51 according to the Below Poverty Line (BPL) criteria. In all there are four different vouchers, one covering tuition costs and the others providing funding for books, uniforms and meals. The tuition voucher amounts to Rs. 4800 ($85.94) per year; uniform Rs. 600 ($10.74 – summer and winter); books Rs. 900 ($16.11) and lunch Rs. 1,000 ($17.91). The total amount per year, per child is Rs. 7300 ($130.71). Children are being funded for five years and the ARK programme is informing government and aid agencies alike, providing them with a framework to follow and build upon as well as the processes needed to implement an education voucher programme in low-income areas and slums of India. The targeted voucher process includes:

- community engagement;
- child identification;
- service implementation;
- private school identification and recruitment;
- voucher and parent handbook design;
- voucher reimbursement process;
- the evaluation and assessment of the effect the voucher has on the individual participants – the randomised control trial.

Figure 4.1   Vouchers from the ARK ENABLE programme

Before the lottery event took place all children that applied were visited in their homes and undertook a Hindi, math and English test. A family background questionnaire was also completed in order to ascertain certain information regarding parental education, assets, employment and expectations.

Some of the poorest children in the slums of Delhi started school in 2011 using ARK vouchers. They are attending schools of their own choice. They applied for the voucher because it meant attaining an education their parents could previously not afford. Because individual vouchers are given directly to parents and each voucher contains, through a barcode, biometric information on each child, there is little room for corrupt activity (see Figure 4.1). Money does not transfer to government officials or bureaucrats. There is total transparency for monetary transfers between ARK, the parent, the voucher provider (Edenred) and the individual private schools. Aid is being given at the very grass-roots level. The money is also supporting the Cheetah generation, supporting businesses and entrepreneurs who are already making a difference for the poor.

At the end of year one of the voucher scheme, children in both control and treatment groups were tested again in the standardised tests. The results show that there is a positive and statistically significant impact of the voucher programme on math achievement. Students in the treatment group scored on average 0.72 points higher on the math assessment, which equals about 0.11 of a standard deviation. There was no statistically significant overall impact of the programme on English or Hindi after one year.

The second study is underway in Andhra Pradesh and is known as the Andhra Pradesh Randomized Evaluation Study (APRESt). In this case three main organisations are involved – the government of Andhra Pradesh (GOAP), the Azim Premji Foundation (APF) and the World Bank.[27] Legatum Global Development is funding the study and evaluation. The design of APRESt involves:

> Offering scholarships that would allow them [poor children] to shift to schools of their choice [if they wish to] in addition to the option of continuing in existing government school. Such a program would provide opportunities for children from disadvantaged families to attend private schools. The research study involves a rigorous evaluation of the impact of school choice both on children who receive the choice as well as on the aggregate impact on education outcomes for all children in the villages where the school choice program is implemented.[28]

Two hundred villages have been identified where private schools operate. Half of these villages were chosen through a randomised lottery allowing for 100 villages to receive vouchers for about 40 children and 100 villages to receive no scholarships. Only children in grades one–three who were currently enrolled in a government school and had not attended a private school could apply. Children would receive the voucher until the end of grade five; therefore the lower the grade at the beginning of the programme the more time the child would have in the study. The voucher amount was set at around the 80th percentile of the private school fee in all villages. Parents were not allowed to top up the fee. The scholarship covered the cost of books, uniform and other school supplies; transport was only covered if the school was not within walking distance. The voucher amount was set at Rs. 3200/- per year (around US$80 per year). The RCT allows for student attainment to be measured and for the treatment and control groups' achievements to be measured over the years of the project. Impact on the community is also being measured by looking at drop-out rates, teacher turnover, changes in pedagogy, if any, attendance rates of pupils and teachers, school fees and other process variables. There is no selection bias to contend with in the data owing to the scholarships being randomly assigned to a subset of potential recipients. Valid comparisons at the village level are also possible owing to the random selection of villages. The programme began in March 2008 and ran until March 2012. Data are still being analysed and reports are forthcoming.

Targeted vouchers are a very good example of an intervention that could improve school access for the poorest. Vouchers could also initially be supported by international aid, and set up by experts in this field.

CASH TRANSFERS – CONDITIONAL AND UNCONDITIONAL

Some, such as Joseph Hanlon et al., suggest that just giving money to the poor is the best solution to ending poverty.[29] In their book *Just Give Money to the Poor*, Hanlon et al. provide evidence from cash transfer programmes around the world, setting out a case to show that cash transfers given direct to the poor are efficient because recipients use the money in a way that best suits their needs. Cash transfers can be unconditional (no conditions attached for gaining the cash) or conditional (the recipients are required to do something to get the cash transfer). They can have a broad target or a narrow target providing a very small or large proportion of household income. Typically, conditional cash transfers (CCTs) request those in receipt of the cash to make specific investments in their children's education and health. The two largest CCTs are in Brazil and Mexico – Bolsa Família and Oportunidades respectively. Chile and Turkey's CCT programmes focus on the extreme poor and socially excluded, and in Bangladesh and Cambodia CCTs aim at reducing gender disparities in education.

The conditions of the CCTs generally require parents to make investments in their children's human capital in the form of healthcare and education. The education condition typically is focused on school enrolment. That is, the child's school attendance requirements are set at between 80 and 85 per cent. Mothers usually receive the transfer and, in addition, some programmes give money to the student.

Looking at the evidence, cash transfers are not only affordable for donors and governments, but provide immediate hardship and poverty reduction for those in receipt of the transfer. They facilitate economic and social development, initiating the potential to reduce long-term poverty. Providing those at the grass roots with a monetary payment, which is regular, assured, practical to administer, fair and politically 'acceptable', allows the poor to be in control and in charge of their own development. Indeed, Hanlon et al. propose that 'instead of maintaining a huge aid industry to find ways to "help the poor", it is better to give money to poor people directly so that they can find their own effective ways to escape from poverty'.[30] 'Cash transfers are not charity or philanthropy but, rather, investments that enable poor people to take control of their own development and end their own poverty.'[31]

Roger Riddell agrees that one way of improving the impact of aid is to 'just give cash to those who need the aid'.[32] That donors typically have not given money to the poor is 'linked to the paternalistic and condescending view that poor people do not know how best to use it'.[33] Championing the use of cash transfers, Riddell suggests that 'on the basis of the evidence, the case for significantly enhancing the impact of aid by giving it directly to poor people would seem to be compelling'.[34]

It would seem from the evidence that providing cash to the poor, even quite small amounts, allows them to transform their own lives:

> Cash transfers are becoming popular precisely because they are tools that can be effectively used for a range of goals, but they are always based on the understanding that it makes sense to give money directly to poor people because they will use it productively and wisely.[35]

Typically, the poor initially spend money on 'immediate' needs, including food and medicine. Once these immediate needs are catered for the next priority are the children; parents using their cash transfers to buy shoes, clothes and school materials. Typically, children, irrespective of the type of cash transfer (for example, pensions, employment, conditional or unconditional), are the main beneficiaries. According to Hanlon et al. 'all cash transfer programs produce an increase in school enrollment and attendance, regardless of conditions and of whether or not such an increase is an explicit goal of the program'.[36]

Examples of Cash Transfers

Goals and priorities set by policy-makers dictate the design of the cash transfer programme. Initially it has to be decided who are the likely beneficiaries of the programme and what the objectives are. There are four main groups that the 'aims' of cash transfer programmes can be divided into:

(1) *Social Protection and Security* – raising the income of the poorest by targeting the young and old, the working poor and helping those who would work but cannot at some point in time (a safety net provision).
(2) *Development and Economic Growth* – stimulating demand typically in the local economy and within the local community. They can also act as security, which promotes investment. Having a guaranteed amount of income each month allows a family to take more risks with regard to the ability to make investments.
(3) *Human Capital and Breaking the Intergenerational Poverty Cycle* – ensuring that children of the poor are healthier, better fed and receive more education than their parents.
(4) *Rights, Equity and Fairness* – providing the poor with a 'right' to an adequate standard of living. Ensuring redistribution from the wealthy to the poor as well as improving the status of women and

giving choice to the poor, which in turn stimulates competition between providers and hence improves efficiency and quality.

It is typical for several of these aims to be included within the design of a cash transfer payment scheme.

One example of a conditional cash transfer scheme that targets schooling is the Oportunidades in Mexico. The grant is divided into different parts. The mother or carer of the children receives a payment, but on top of this so do children in the household who attend school more than 85 per cent of the time. Food supplements and medicines are also given free. On average the family cash transfer is $30 per month and the in-kind transfers $6 per month. Money can be spent in any way the recipients wish.[37] The research evidence suggests that teenagers who benefit from Oportunidades are 33 per cent more likely to be enrolled in middle and junior high school, and 23 per cent more likely to complete grade nine than those not receiving cash transfers through the programme.

Another CCT targeting schooling is Colombia's child benefit CCT–Familias en Acción, which targets around 1.7 million households, providing a grant of between $8 and $33 per child, which is dependent on age and conditional on the child attending school and a medical clinic. A third example is Panama's Red de Oportunidades, which is a CCT scheme aimed at around 50,000 of the poorest households, providing $35 per month. The grant is conditional on children attending school and medical clinics and mothers attending human development lessons.

Those CCT programmes that focus on secondary education include the Bangladesh Female Secondary School Assistance Program (FSSAP), Cambodia's Japan Fund for Poverty Reduction (JFPR) and the Cambodia Education Sector Support Project (CESSP). Primary school focus is given by CCTs in Bolivia and Kenya and all schooling is the focus of the Jaring Pengamanan Sosial (JPS) CCT in Indonesia and with the Social Risk Mitigation Project in Turkey. Others include the Punjab Education Sector Reform Program in Pakistan, targeting girls aged 10–14 years, and the Bono de Desarrollo Humano (BDH) in Ecuador.

In Bangladesh, Pakistan and Turkey, CCTs have contributed to the reduction in gender disparity where initially more boys attended school than girls. This gender gap has been reduced by these programmes. The Eduque a la Niña programme of Guatemala also provides scholarships to girls. Findings show that those receiving the scholarship are more likely to attend school regularly and less likely to repeat grades. An unintended consequence of the scholarship was that boys in schools where girls on scholarships were attending were more likely to experience similar gains in achievement and attendance. Benefits of CCTs in Bogotá, Colombia, show that children are more likely to attend school, remain enrolled and to matriculate to the next grade.[38]

However, although school enrolment and attendance typically increase when families are in receipt of cash transfers, there have been issues with programmes where children have not been supported by the schools and 'dumped in the back of the classrooms'.[39] In the Brazilian Bolsa Família cash transfer programme it was found that although the programme was shown to improve life chances of children, reduce poverty and inequality, children did not improve their educational outcomes:

> The failure of Bolsa Família and other cash transfers to improve educational outcomes is often attributed to teachers not paying special attention to children from poor families who joined their classes ... simply sending a poor child to school is not very useful; the quality of the education offered must be high enough to ensure that the child learns.[40]

And, according to the World Bank:

> In country after country, school enrollment has increased among CCT beneficiaries – especially among the poorest children, whose enrollment rates at the outset were the lowest.[41]

But, the impact on final educational outcomes such as achievement and cognitive development is 'mixed',[42] and 'there is little evidence of improvements in learning outcomes'.[43]

Two evaluations on student outcomes undertaken on Oportunidades in Mexico[44] and BDH in Ecuador[45] showed there to be no significant effect of the CCT programme on test scores. What this is saying is that children who take up schooling because of the CCT learn no less than children who are accessing schooling without it. Two extra years of schooling gained through the Oportunidades programme had no effect on language and math tests. Those with a shorter exposure to the transfers did just as well.[46] Rather worryingly, looking at data from the Mexico CCT programme, even after controlling for socio-economic background and school quality, 'receiving an Oportunidades scholarship is negatively and significantly related to achievement'.[47]

Why might this be the case? Again according to the World Bank one possibility is that 'the quality of services is so low, perhaps especially for the poor, that increased use alone does not yield large benefits'.[48] It is recognised that:

> In many developing countries, the delivery of education and health services is dysfunctional. Poor infrastructure, absenteeism, and lack of adequate supplies

are not unusual problems in schools and health centers. Achieving the human capital goals of CCT programs will require adaptation of the supply of services. In some countries, this adaptation may require governments or other actors to provide services where none existed before.[49]

And

> schools particularly fail the disadvantaged children who are induced to enroll by a CCT, perhaps because the curricula and pedagogical methods used are geared toward relatively more advanced students.[50]

The quality of schooling for those being provided a CCT is raising concerns, 'issues of quality of instruction, teacher education and school management are virtually left out of the theoretical frameworks of CCT programmes'.[51] And yes, those who receive CCTs are more likely to be segregated into (up until now) government schools that on average offer lower quality. Another difficulty is the management of the CCT programme. Typically, the government manages CCTs, often remotely from education ministries; 'this remote control is at the heart of some of the conceptual deficiencies ... CCT programmes do not address direct improvements in the quality of education, because the units overseeing them have no functional authority over schools'.[52]

The answer, therefore, could be low-cost private schools. Up until now it could be safe to suggest that schools that have been accessed via CCTs and CTs in general have been government ones. In India this would not be the case. Cash transfers could be one way to provide the poorest parents with a choice to access low-cost private schools in India, and indeed other developing countries, allowing children to benefit from their higher standards with regard to quality and activity of teaching. If low-cost private schools already exist then parents would have that choice. Where they do not already exist then the market would, eventually, encourage entrepreneurs to set up low-cost private schools to cater for the new demand in new areas. In order to attract students and their additional fee income paid out of the CT, private schools need to provide these students with an education for them to remain in their school. Thus dispelling the problems concerning the detachment of government from education ministries. It is the market that will maintain standards, owing to the need to attract students. Parents will keep the private schools accountable.

How To Do It

In order for a cash transfer programme to operate there needs to be a method of establishing the eligibility of the clients alongside a framework for enrolling them into the programme. Following from that a mechanism is required in order to pay the benefit. CCTs require monitoring for compliance with the condition. Ideally monitoring and evaluation should be part of the whole scheme.

Targeting the poor or poorest can be carried out by using a geographical focus (that is, low income and slum areas), followed by household vetting. It has to be ascertained what the criteria for eligibility is, setting cut-off points for those who do and do not qualify. As the programme's aim is to increase access to private schooling then obviously parents with children of the predetermined age and/or gender are included in the targeting process. However targeting and monitoring obviously increase the cost of the programme and hence reduce the programme's cost efficiency. Not targeting implies money going to those who do not need it, which will imply less impact and effectiveness. Targeting in this case would be the most effective; not only of the poorest, but those unable to access private schooling where they desire it.

Once targeting has been decided, then determining the amount of the transfer is crucial. Aid agencies using cash transfers to promote the opportunity for poor parents to choose a low-cost private school for their child would *not* necessarily need to choose a CCT type. Evidence shows that when giving money to the poor they prioritise their own spending, with children being the main beneficiaries of the grants, irrespective of their target. Research shows that children are the main beneficiaries of cash transfers, irrespective of their type; so any form of giving money to the poor that is targeted in respect to poverty would allow the poorest parents to access education for their children. In Brazil the main increases in spending are on food, children's clothing, children's healthcare and education.[53] Hanlon et al. state that this is typical, with half the grant spent on more, better and more varied food, after which children's clothing and shoes become the next monetary priority.

Owing to the proliferation of low-cost private schools, typically in rural and urban India, just giving money to the poor could allow them to be able to make choices regarding school access.

Means testing would be preferred, as those who can afford to send their children to low-cost private schools are already doing so. In Mexico, for example, poor households were identified using a point system based on the family members' age, gender, education, whether the house had electricity and tap water and whether the family owned certain assets such as a radio, television and bicycle. Receiving money could be through electronic means or collected from shops, banks, post offices, cash machines or mobile cash units. In Brazil payments are made on a debit card and cash is withdrawn in banks, at cash machines or at lottery sales outlets. In

Turkey payments are made by the state bank in cash; in Mexico until quite recently cash was paid in temporary payment points, such as in community centres; and in Kenya a new method using mobile phone technology has been trialled.

When giving cash transfers it would be initially beneficial if there were a high proliferation of private schools providing quality education in the area. If schools were not available then it could be assumed that poor parents now having cash through the cash transfer would demand schooling and this would instigate or initiate entrepreneurs to set up schools to cater for this new demand and clientele.

FROM BOOTSTRAP FINANCING TO IMPACT INVESTING

The market for low-cost private schools is demand driven. Competition between the affordable private schools is fierce. Retaining and attracting pupils is a high priority for the school entrepreneur. Many are looking to improve their school's quality and expand capacity. In the majority of places, however, operating within a slum implies no property rights. No deeds or collateral to secure a loan.

In India it is against the law to make a 'profit' from education. Therefore school accounts cannot show the true state of the school's ability to pay back any financial advances. Gaining a loan to improve one's school has in the past been almost impossible. Bootstrap financing has until quite recently been the only way the affordable private schools could expand and improve. There was no external funding available. In some cases school entrepreneurs would, and still do, use a 'chit' fund type arrangement to finance growth; a group of school owners (forming a 'federation') putting money in a pot used by each of them in turn to facilitate advancement.

The lack of available capital has been a barrier that has retarded the progress and growth of the affordable private schools' sector in developing countries. But owing to the light shone on these private schools over the last decade a new industry has sprung up revolving specifically around low-cost private schools.

Impact investors – those looking for a financial return to their investment but who are also taking into account the social and environmental impact the business will have owing to the investment – have emerged. The supply of capital for low-cost private schools can now be accessed through companies such as Gray Ghost Ventures, Edify, Opportunity International and the IDP Foundation who are now investing in the affordable private school space.

Gray Matters Capital Foundation (GMC) and Gray Ghost Ventures (GGV) work in Hyderabad, India, to provide market based capital solutions for entrepreneurs addressing the needs of low-income families. GMC and GGV act as an impact investor, catalytic donor or co-creator, depending on the requirements of the entrepreneurs. In 2009 Gray Ghost Ventures started the Indian School Finance Company (ISFC). Operating out of Hyderabad the ISFC provides capital to affordable private schools across India. The loans are repaid at market interest rates. The minimum amount available is 5 lakh rupees (Rs. 500,000, approximately $8953) with an average loan taken by the school owners of 12 lakh rupees (Rs. 1,200,000/-, $21,486). Repayment timescales run from one–five years and the school owners need to provide proof of collateral or a guarantor that covers the loan. Loans are typically utilised to improve infrastructure. The ISFC aims to provide school owners with the capital they need to improve their academic quality with the ability to do so for more children owing to expansion. The ISFC is also carrying out a programme with school owners that allows them to improve their ability and capacity to utilise loan capital in a productive and cost-effective way. By 2011, the ISFC had provided 250 loans to low-cost private schools.[54] The main issues regarding expansion for the ISFC are associated with the lack of formal accounts held by low-cost private schools. This leads to difficulties when making a credit evaluation and leads to subjective due diligence. Lending decisions are often based on intuition and gut feeling rather than process efficiency. Interest rates are high at 20 per cent or more owing to the high risk of lending, operation and processing costs in the sector.[55]

Edify work with microfinance partners in the Dominican Republic and Ghana, making loans to low-cost private schools at 'competitive' rates of interest that are 'in many cases lower than commercial bank rates'.[56] As of 2011 a total of 440 Edify loans worth a total of US$3 million were assisting affordable private schools. In Ghana the average loan amount is roughly US$2800. Typically loans are used to improve infrastructure. It has been necessary for Edify to employ fully dedicated accountants to work with and visit each Edify loan school at least once a month to review the books and cash flow. Early detection of the inability to repay is essential. Edify is targeting providing loans to around 4000 schools by 2016, impacting at least one million children.

The IDP Foundation Inc. (cofounder and president being Irene Pritzker), in conjunction with Ghanaian microfinance institutions Sinapi Aba Trust (SAT) and Opportunity International, set up the IDP Rising Schools Program in Ghana in 2009. The IDP Foundation provides financial and capacity building services to low-cost private schools in Ghana.

As of 2011, IDP was working with 103 private schools in Ghana. School owners, before they can access loans, are required to take a 12-module course on financial literacy and school management.

Opportunity International, also working in Ghana, has set up an initiative known as 'Banking on Education' which provides loans to school entrepreneurs for infrastructure, expansion and in some cases to start schools. As of 2011 Opportunity International were working with around 500 low-cost private schools.

Loans are allowing schools to improve their quality and to benefit from economies of scale. This is a scalable and sustainable solution for raising quality standards as well as the expansion of the low-cost private schools' market.

However, regulations need to be less restrictive for microfinance companies and businesses entering these markets. Multiple regulatory hoops are causing barriers to entry for impact investors, impeding growth within the sector. In India affordable private schools should also be allowed by law to make profits. Profits pertain to efficiency, innovation and effectiveness. The inability to legally show profits is detrimental to the sector.

Some private school owners are demanding large loans but, owing to the lack of competition between microfinance companies, in some cases they are being denied access to the amounts they require. Opening up these markets can only be better for everyone. It is a win-win situation for the impact investors, the children, parents, teachers, school owners and the communities themselves. International aid agencies could focus on the improvement and relaxation of regulations for the loan market for low-cost private schools.

RTE AND REGULATION – ACCREDITATION AGENCIES

The Right of Children to Free and Compulsory Education Act or the 'Right to Education Act' (RTE) came into force in the spring of 2010. According to some the RTE marked a historic moment because children in India are now 'guaranteed their right' to 'quality' elementary education by the state.

As already considered in Chapter 3, both recognised and unrecognised private schools exist in India, where recognised schools purportedly operate within the on-paper rules and laws and the latter do not.

Recognition is granted when a private school abides by both the rules and laws set out by the individual state and the central government. These rules and regulations are extensive. Generally they are too stringent, focusing on inputs and elements that have been shown by research not to lead to higher pupil outcomes or improve quality.[57] The attainment of such requirements in many cases is impossible for low-cost PUA schools to attain – large playgrounds, high teacher qualification and salary levels comparable to those paid in government schools, substantial numbers of books in the library, and so on. Luxuries are not affordable by low-cost private schools funded mainly by student fees running on a small budget. For example, providing teachers with inflated wages and following the salary scale of the government, which have been negotiated by teacher unions and paid by the government to public school teachers, would make private schools no longer affordable by the poor.

But still these low-cost private schools gain recognition irrespective of whether they meet the regulations or not. For example, making a profit from education is against the law; in practice school owners report that this is widely ignored. Although there is a multitude of regulations governing all aspects of a school's work, in practice they are ignored too.

The rules and laws are substantive. However, when government officials were asked how many rules private school owners in Hyderabad have to abide by to gain recognition the response was quite bizarre and completely wrong. District Education Officers (DEOs) believed that only four needed to be met.[58] However, looking at the rules as well as the schools it is quite clear that even if we consider only those four regulations the majority of recognised private schools only meet two of the four. So how do these schools gain recognition? Why do the DEOs not know how many rules and regulations private schools are required to meet in order to gain recognition?

The main issue is the culture of bribery and corruption. There are too few inspectors, and the ones that operate expect private school owners to provide them with either monetary returns or gifts when they grant recognition or visit to ensure standards are being maintained. Enforcement of regulations is impossible because they are not focused on improving the quality of schooling and they are generally not affordable by low-cost private schools. According to one DEO in Hyderabad 'the whole system is corrupt there is no way of checking up on the schools. There are only three inspectors for all of these schools in Hyderabad'.[59]

School owners are quite candid about why DEOs visit low-cost private schools so regularly – they come to take a bribe. Inspectors spend time in the school owner's office, discussing 'business' without looking at the facilities or visiting classrooms to observe teaching. School owners believe that if they did not bribe and had to follow the 'proper' channels every path would be closed to them and applications would never be processed.

Indeed this is very typical of the processes entrepreneurs go through in developing countries in all types of businesses.[60]

What is really important to private school owners is dealing with consumer demand and meeting the needs of parents. Because fees are low and schools are running on a tight budget, they need to employ cost-effective measures to maximise profit levels, or at least surpluses, and to allow the fees to remain affordable to those living in the locality.

The private school entrepreneurs have found that student achievement levels are not hindered by their apparent 'disregard' for the 'on-paper' rules and therefore an extra-legal sector runs parallel, where school owners are driven by what works rather than what the government thinks private schools should provide and in what measures. Entrepreneurs buy official regulations with a bribe and proceed with their own self-regulating strategy, following their own rules through the accountability they have to parents and the desire to maximise profits. The 'on-paper' regulations are ignored, even when they are brought down to the four that DEOs believe the schools should abide by! The low-cost private school industry is a prosperous, thriving, innovative industry answerable not to the government but to the consumer, the parent.

So why do schools need to apply for and gain recognition? What are the benefits recognition brings to the school and the children? The major motivation for the school is that when recognised the pupils are able, through the school, to take the state exams. Without recognition status the school cannot offer state examinations. Also, children are required to possess or be given a transfer certificate when moving between schools, thus providing them with the ability to gain access not only to a private school, but also a government one. Without recognition private schools cannot issue transfer certificates. Interestingly, recognised schools charge higher fees than unrecognised ones, implying a bigger surplus possibility for the owner; even when parents are asked, they do not often know whether their child's school is recognised or not. Some schools do not want to be recognised because of the implications this brings, including visits from government officials. The visits imply extra cost, brought about by having to bribe the officials each time. Unrecognised schools also include those waiting to gain recognition and those that have just been founded. The recognition process is often very slow and, again, in order for papers and application materials to be moved to the next department, bribes are required to all dealing with its advancement.

On 1 April 2010, the Right of Children to Free and Compulsory Education Act, 2009, came into force in India. The RTE Act has provided state governments with an opportunity to consider ways to ensure that rules and laws focus on stimulating and maintaining quality. The Act also stipulates that children between the ages of six and 14 years have a right to free and compulsory education 'in a neighbourhood school' without paying fees.

PUA schools are required to reserve 25 per cent of their places for children from the poorest families. Their fees are to be reimbursed by the state as part of a public–private partnership operation. However, there are obviously foreseeable problems, including whether schools have the capacity to cater for these children and whether fees are going to be effectively and efficiently transferred from government to low-cost private schools? In all honesty, probably not.

All unrecognised schools according to the RTE are prohibited to practice. That is, all PUA schools need to be recognised by 2013, otherwise they will be closed down. A large proportion of affordable private schools currently remain outside the law. Forcing them to close owing to the RTE implies hundreds of thousands of children without a school to attend. When testing around 6000 children in different school management types in Delhi and Hyderabad, private unrecognised schools outperformed government ones in math, English and Hindi; all this at a fraction of the teacher cost as detailed in Chapter 3. In theory, and taking into consideration much of the research, if these displaced children are to access government schools they will be heading for a school that offers lower quality provision. In reality government schools do not have the capacity to take on such an influx of children. The question has to be asked, how does the government propose to raise the education budget to take these children on in government schools?

The recognition norms as set out in the RTE and the Model Rules Under the Right of Children to Free and Compulsory Education Act, 2009, are specified below. States have to also come up with their own rules for the implementation of the RTE.

The Gujarat RTE Rules are also considered. Why Gujarat? Gujarat is one of the only states placing emphasis on learning outcomes rather than specific input requirements. According to Parth Shah of the Centre for Civil Society, Gujarat is making some path-breaking rules that could set a precedent for other states to follow.[61]

The Norms and Standards for Schools – RTE

Private school owners had to initially submit a self-declaration to their DEO which stated that their school complied with the norms and standards as set out in the Schedule at the back of the RTE Act and other conditions as set out in the Model Rules Under the Right of Children to Free and Compulsory Education Act, 2009, and the RTE. The self-declaration included the need to provide information on:

- total income and expenditure for the last three years showing surplus/deficit;
- medium of instruction;
- total area of the schools;
- enrolment numbers;
- the size of the kitchen;
- requires an attached list of sports and play equipment;
- number of books in the library;
- number of periodicals and newspapers in the library;
- types of WC and urinals;
- number of boys' and number of girls' lavatories;
- all the particulars of every teaching member of staff including academic qualification, teaching experience, training and professional qualifications;
- details of the curriculum and syllabus followed up to Class VIII;
- systems of pupil assessment.

The declaration also implied that the school did not run for-profit (Model Rules 11(1)(b)).

After the receipt of the declaration on the appropriate FORM 1 paperwork, an on-site inspection was to be carried out by the DEO, which, if the school passed, would imply provisional recognition for a three-year period. If the DEO deemed the school not to comply with the norms, standards and conditions as set out by the RTE and Schedule, the school was put on a list through a public order and could reapply for another on-site inspection. However the time period to do this was within three years. If the inspection failed again, then the school would have to 'cease to function' (Model Rules 11(6)). Some of the norms and standards set out by the RTE include those regarding teachers, school buildings and pupil–teacher ratios, hence input requirements rather than learning outcomes. Those private schools that do not adhere to the rules face the threat of closure. Chapter IV, section 18, sub-section (5) states that:

> Any person who establishes or runs a school without obtaining certificate of recognition, or continues to run a school after withdrawal of recognition, shall be liable to fine which may extend to one lakh rupees and in case of continuing contraventions, to a fine of ten thousand rupees for each day during which such contravention continues (RTE Clause 18(5)).

There are multiple stipulations regarding teachers. Teachers may only be appointed if they have the minimum qualification 'as laid down by an academic authority, authorised by the Central Government' (RTE section 23(1)). Where teachers do not conform to the 'minimum' qualification they need to gain this within five years (RTE section 23(3)). As stated in the Model Rules Under the Right of Children to Free and Compulsory Education Act, 2009, (MR) 'a person appointed as a teacher within six months of the commencement of the Act, must possess at least the academic qualifications not lower than higher secondary school certificate or equivalent' (MR – 16(6), p. 10).

The salary of the teachers, as well as allowances and terms and conditions of service, 'shall be such as may be prescribed' (RTE section 23(3)). According to the MR:

> the scales of pay and allowances, medical facilities, pension, gratuity, provident fund, and other prescribed benefits of teachers, including those employed for the purpose of imparting special training as specified in Section 4, shall be that of regular teachers, and at par for similar work and experience (18(3)).

Teachers are also required to teach the curriculum within the specified time (RTE section 24(1c)) and in the medium of instruction as per the 'child's mother tongue' (RTE section 29(2f)). Teachers are forbidden to be involved in any private teaching activity (RTE section 28). The Schedule sets out the minimum number of days and hours to be worked in an academic year and sets the minimum working hours per week for teachers at 45 (RTE Sl. No.3&4).

Pupil–teacher ratios are set out as per the size of the private school. The minimum for Classes I to V being 30:1 in schools below 200 and in those above 200 children the pupil–teacher ratio must not exceed 40:1. For schools catering for Classes VI to VIII there needs to be a teacher for each subject, a maximum pupil–teacher ratio of 35:1. Where there are more than 100 children in the school the head teacher is required to be full-time. Part-time instructors need to be employed to teach art, health and physical education (PE) (RTE Norm 1(b)(1–3)).

Schools are required to provide a playground, separate toilets for boys and girls, drinking water, a kitchen, barrier-free access and a classroom for every teacher (RTE Sl. 2(i)–(vi)). A school library is also necessary in which newspapers, magazines and books (on all subjects) are provided (RTE Sl. No.6).

The RTE focuses on inputs rather than considering the outcomes of schooling. Private schools are being penalised for not having the inputs required by the RTE, even though, generally, they are providing children with schooling that stimulates learning outcomes. State governments have to draft state rules under the Model Rules proposed by the central government. It could be easy to propose that state governments will set out rules that become too prescriptive and too detailed, targeting inputs that do not have a positive impact on efficiency and student outcomes. According to a report from the IFC the:

> regulation of private education must seek to ensure high quality delivery, while at the same time encouraging investment ... the regulatory and funding frameworks in many countries do little to provide an enabling operating environment that promotes growth in private education.[62]

The study sets out propositions for good practice in regulatory and registration regimes including:

- explicitly articulating the role of the private sector in articulating educational goals;
- regulatory requirements that are output focused – that is they do not impose fixed national norms or ratios but ask open questions about standards which allows flexibility;
- an accreditation process with accreditation agencies that set performance targets and limits on providing reports and responses to schools;
- a greater role for private sector organisations in the regulation and registration process;
- publishing reports from independent or accrediting agencies about the performance of private schools to ensure transparency;
- an independent quality assurance monitoring mechanism to evaluate the performance and programme outcomes of private and public education providers;
- the contracting out of monitoring and quality assurance accreditation to charitable organisations or private sector companies.

There has been an opportunity to change how the state governments see regulation and recognition for PUA schools, incorporating some of the good practices as has already been suggested by the IFC report. Indeed, as already suggested, the state of Gujarat is moving forward with some innovative ideas with its Rules for the Implementation of the Right to Education Act (RTE) 2009. The Gujarat RTE Rules are emphasising student learning outcomes rather than input requirements. Accordingly, in order to gain recognition, the Gujarat Rules set out a formula made up of an average of four measures:

(1) student learning outcomes (absolute levels) – 30 per cent weighting;
(2) student learning outcomes (improvement compared to the school's past performance) – 40 per cent weighting;

(3)   student non-academic outcomes (co-curricular and sports, personality and values) and parent feedback – 15 per cent weighting;
(4)   inputs (including facilities, teacher qualifications) – 15 per cent weighting.

Independent assessment using standardised tests will determine the students' level of learning to consider absolute levels. A baseline in year one will be established for each school in order to determine the improvements of the school's performance in subsequent years. Parental feedback will be gathered from a random sample of parents across the different grades provided by the school. The Gujarat Rules are therefore corresponding with the propositions for good practice in regulatory and registration regimes as proposed by the likes of the IFC. According to Parth Shah:

> This is one of the first times in India's history that public policy has focused on children and parents, instead of focusing on the public sector producers of education services.[63]

Other innovative ideas include rules on facilities that are not set out in absolute terms, but where the classroom area is small a formula is provided to determine pupil–teacher ratios in smaller spaces. As already noted, the RTE Act forces schools to close down if they cannot meet the regulatory requirements. However in Gujarat, management of a de-recognised school can be transferred to a third party or the state, allowing the school to continue and strive to meet the norms.

The state of Gujarat has recognised, through this approach, the contribution that low-cost private schools are making to provide education for children and parents in the state. International aid agencies can look at how independent assessments can be undertaken, working with those already practicing in this area, such as GMC in India, and international assessor and evaluators, such as the Centre for British Teachers (CfBT). There could also be a role for federations to become more active in the assessment and evaluation process and criteria.

Corruption is endemic in India. India is ranked among the top ten most corrupt nations in the world. However, if the regulations governing the PUA sector were fewer, flexible and outcome driven, in line with the Gujarat proposals, corruption would be more difficult, thus allowing recognition and evaluations to be meaningful and thus providing parents with information that reflects the true state of each school. Where private organisers are undertaking assessments and evaluations it is less likely that bribery and corruption can take a widespread hold. A strong stance, such as instant dismissal accompanied by public humiliation, would need to be taken on any employee, individual or team, found to accept bribes from schools in order for them to gain a better evaluation or recognition.

Independent Assessment and Evaluation

A pilot rating system for PUA schools has been trialled in Hyderabad, Andhra Pradesh. GMC set up the pilot 'rating system' to help address the 'information problem'[64] faced by parents when trying to choose a low-cost private school for their children. Recognition received from the government does not differentiate between the quality of private schools owing to the inadequacy of the regulations as well as the corruption associated with gaining recognition. In conjunction with a micro-credit-rating agency (M-CRIL), it conducted an initial pilot of ten schools in 2009.

The rating system, which according to GMC, the philanthropic foundation of Gray Ghost Ventures, is affordable, assesses schools in terms of their quality of provision compared to other providers in the neighbourhood and against local and national norms. As the rating system becomes more widespread it is hoped that it will provide parents with the information they require to make more informed choices and supply investors with details they need when seeking school investment opportunities. GMC could also now be one of the independent assessors in states like Gujarat. The rating tool is made up of six categories:

(1) Student Learning Outcomes – grade specific tests in English and maths for grades 3, 5, 7 and 9.
(2) Parent Satisfaction – parental surveys measuring satisfaction on infrastructure, management and academics.
(3) Teaching Quality – classroom observations and teacher tests in English and maths.
(4) School Management – Teacher satisfaction on management practices and school leader interview.
(5) Financial Performance – revenue courses and cost drivers.
(6) School Infrastructure – audit of infrastructure assessing basic amenities and infrastructures.

The rating provides an objective perspective to the school owner concerning their school and provides feedback concerning areas that can be improved. A sample of the children undertakes tests, and focus groups are held with a random sample of teachers, parents and other school stakeholders. Observations are also carried out throughout the school in order to consider the overall environment. Investigations into the school's financial sustainability and viability are also undertaken. A detailed school assessment report is provided to the school leader once the data analysis has been carried out and a school report card (SRC) shares the ratings with parents. The assessment report allows the school owner to identify gaps in the school's performance, and for parents the SRC allows them to monitor school performance. In 2011–2012 around 202 low-cost private schools were evaluated in Hyderabad, paying about Rs. 7000/- ($126) for the evaluation to take place and to receive a report on how their school compares to others operating in the sector along with their specific school evaluation. In order to encourage low-cost private schools to participate, GMC provides a voucher in the School Improvement Voucher Program (SIVP), which is worth around Rs. 20,000/- (US$400), to be spent on educational supplies shown to have had an impact on learning. Products are displayed and vouchers cashed during a GMC-organised one-day event. The average cost of the school rating is Rs. 30,000/- (around US$600) per school; however, this has been offered at a subsidised rate, so in Hyderabad in the first year the ratings were subsidised by 80 per cent, falling to 50 per cent in year two. However, 200 schools underwent a repeat rating in year two.

Others who could compete in a market of evaluation and assessment companies include CfBT and the Sindh Education Foundation. CfBT has been carrying out inspections on behalf of Ofsted for almost 20 years. The aim is to provide a high quality school inspection, which results in the improvement of the school involved. CfBT are one of the first major providers of inspection services in the UK. The Sindh Education Foundation in Pakistan operates the Support to Private Education Institution Programme (SPEIP), which provides support 'as part of a wider school improvement strategy in the private sector'.[65] Within the SPEIP an assessment system concerning performance for private schools is being established. The objectives include:

- To devise mechanisms among private schools and districts for training support.
- To design a meticulous framework for process support, quality improvement and continuous accountability of private and religious education providers.
- To launch meaningful research projects to build the models for low-cost and high quality institutions of learning.

With the introduction of the RTE comes an opportunity to stimulate the efficiency and effectiveness of PUA schools through a new regulatory model such as the one being proposed by the state of Gujarat. Such regulatory and evaluation strategies as set out in the chapter could be one way forward for improving and monitoring the quality of PUA schools in India, moving regulatory authority from the state to private interest groups. International aid agencies could assist in the growth of competing private school ratings and evaluation agencies and stimulate the environment in which they operate.

CHAINS OF LOW-COST PRIVATE SCHOOLS

As in other industries, the provision of goods and services around the world has benefitted from the emergence of brands and chains within markets. Walking into a pharmacy provided by Walmart or a furniture store like Ikea in any country around the world, the consumer is aware of the type of service and products that will be available. Buying a MacBook Air in Newcastle's Apple store and taking it for repair in New York or Amsterdam, one is assured of the quality of service, irrespective of where in the world the outlet is. The brand is paramount, as is the protection of that brand and its continual promotion. The Apple store in Newcastle has staff trained by Apple, knowledgeable of the products and services on offer, just as the staff are in New York.

The growth of most businesses implies being able to benefit from economies of scale. Growth allows companies to operate more efficiently owing to the increase in size and it provides consumers with knowledge through branding. Economies of scale include the ability to have greater purchasing power thorough bulk buying, to benefit from specialisation in managerial ability, being able to obtain lower interest charges on loans, having greater access to marketing and media markets as well as taking advantage of technology. There are also diseconomies of scale that can arise when a business becomes too big and issues regarding bureaucratic complications arise.

The Evidence

There is very little research evidence concerning the performance of chains of schools compared to individually run ones in developing countries. Most of the research has been carried out in the US looking at Charter schools. However, a report by Gregory Elacqua et al. sets out to determine the 'optimal' scale for the operation of schools, taking data from Chile.[66] Previous research from the US shows that schools that are members of large franchises can benefit from sound institutional environments and that chains of schools have a greater ability to raise investment for expansion as well as to gain credibility and acceptability within their communities.[67] However there are those that believe diseconomies of scale can set in when school organisations become too large and bureaucratic.[68] Indeed there is a small school movement in the US, which recently benefitted (in 2010) from funding from Bill and Melinda Gates, who provided through their foundation more than $1 billion, partly to create 197 small high schools in New York City.[69]

The research from Chile considers grade four children's achievement in both private and government primary schools, which are funded through the national voucher scheme.[70] In 2008 just over half of the children in Chile attended private schools, 48 per cent through vouchers and 7 per cent in non-voucher elite private schools. In Chile 70 per cent of private voucher schools are independent and do not belong to a franchise, 88 per cent of all independent schools are for-profit, with only 12 per cent non-profit secular, Protestant and Catholic schools.

A franchise is where a school belongs to a network of private schools operated by the same owner, and these account for just under one-third of Chile's private schools, with the majority of franchises being made up of fewer than four schools. There are both for-profit and non-profit voucher schools. For-profit franchises are typically run by groups of local entrepreneurs and are typically funded through private shareholders.[71] With 70 per cent of private voucher schools being independent, only 30 per cent are in a franchise. For-profit franchise private voucher primary schools account for around 42 per cent of the franchise schools with the remaining being non-profit franchises, made up of Catholic, Protestant and secular run schools. The math and Spanish test scores of 245,607 fourth grade students attending government, voucher franchise and voucher independent primary schools were analysed. These show, after controlling for selection bias, as well as peer and individual attributes, that children attending private voucher franchise schools outperform those in both government and independent voucher schools in both math and Spanish. There is a positive and significant private voucher franchise school effect of 0.086 standard deviations in Spanish and 0.094 standard deviations in math over private voucher independent schools. Private voucher independent schools outperform public schools, where government schools are performing significantly worse in Spanish by −0.037 standard deviation and negatively in math, but the difference is not significant.[72] But what about the size of the franchise, does this have an effect on children's achievement? The data show that children in a franchise of four or more schools outperform other students having a 'substantial advantage (between 0.11 and 0.18 standard deviation) over private voucher independent schools than private voucher schools that belong to smaller franchises of two or three schools (0.07 to 0.09 standard deviation)'.[73] It was also found that the effect is not correlated with religious affiliation. All franchise schools outperform private independent voucher schools. As described above this could be because of the:

> substantial benefits of scale of educational professionals and administrators, the bulk purchase of supplies and equipment, and the costs of implementing innovations in curriculum. Private schools franchises may also be more likely to benefit from access to credit and private investment than smaller private independent schools in Chile.[74]

The findings from Chile imply that 'policies oriented to create incentives for schools to establish franchises or to be managed by an organization that runs a network of schools may have potential for increasing educational outcomes'.[75]

Examples of Chains of Low-Cost Private Schools

One option for aid and funding could be to encourage competing low-cost chains of private schools. Currently there are only a handful of low-cost chains around the world, which include the Omega chain in Ghana, Empathy Learning Systems in India and Bridge Schools in Kenya.

The first Bridge school opened at the start of 2009. Currently Bridge International Academies has established a network of around 70 low-cost private schools around Nairobi, Kenya, with a view to opening 400 in the chain. The schools' construction is from wood, corrugated steel and iron mesh, the cost to build one classroom is around $1800, and fees are about $4 per month. All lessons are scripted, word-by-word, minute-by-minute, teachers are imparting knowledge at the same time. Teachers are also paid more for better performance and less if achievement does not rise and the same goes for school managers.

Omega Schools opened its first school in 2010 and operates in Ghana. A for-profit chain, currently of ten schools and providing schooling for around 6000 students, it charges a daily fee of 1 cedi (around 60 cents). The children pay a daily fee, which is much easier for parents to afford than saving up for a whole month or termly fee. The fee includes lunch, uniform, books and tuition. According to Omega Schools, sending a child to a government school in Ghana costs at least 90 per cent of the private fee. So, in total, the government school would cost around 54 cents owing to the hidden charges in government schools, such as exam fees, uniform, books, parent–teacher association fees, and so on.

The schools use the same model as any fee-paying low-cost private school. Making a surplus, each school in the chain provides part of the surplus it makes to maintain and fund the chain's head office. This implies not only benefits from economies of scale, but the chain can afford to work on curriculum and pedagogy development and devise and evaluate different methods of testing and assessments. When schools are working as individuals, this is not possible, although benefits through joining a federation could be comparable to some extent. Parents know what they are getting from the brand and this branding along with maintaining excellence within the brand is imperative.

The potential of chains of low-cost private schools has been recognised by Pearson, an education company operating in 70 countries who also own the *Financial Times* and Penguin. In 2012 they launched a fund of $15 million in order to invest in quality education for the poor. The fund – The Pearson Affordable Learning Fund – 'aims to build scalable services to meet a burgeoning demand for affordable education services in Africa, Asia and elsewhere'. The fund is going to invest in and provide support to organisations that focus on education solutions for the poor; this could include accreditation, teacher training and mobile technology provision of educational content. The first investment announced in July 2012 is to the Omega chain of low-cost private schools in Ghana. The aim is to assist in the expansion of the chain, from its current ten schools serving 6000 children, to one 'serving tens of thousands of students throughout Ghana'.[76] Pearson already invests in Bridge International Academies in Kenya. Sir Michael Barber is the Chairman of the Fund and Pearson's Chief Education Advisor. International agencies could provide other investments to help those wishing to expand or provide training to federations. Research could be funded to learn more about any costs or benefits low-cost chains of private schools might bring to the market.

INNOVATIVE PEDAGOGY FOR TEACHING AND LEARNING – LET THE MARKET DECIDE

Learning in low-cost private schools is typically by rote. There is nothing wrong in that under the circumstances, especially as rote learning is tailored to get children through the state exams, which typically focus on memory ability. But learning could be focused on so much more, stimulating creativity and thinking skills as well as group, partner and individual work. Learning could be inspiring as well as enquiring, so that learners are able to ask lots of questions. Being creative, challenging and encouraging learners to want to know more, is beneficial to all students and teachers. Teachers that encourage thinking in a critical and collaborative way rather that just learning something off by heart or by rote is certainly something to aim for.

In low-cost private schools in India interventions have been carried out, both in Hyderabad and Delhi, to investigate methods that would improve the delivery of English, using some of the inspiring and enquiring learning techniques mentioned above. When low-cost private school owners were asked what they wanted help with they indicated their English curriculum and improving children's ability to speak, read and write English. In India this is particularly important owing to low-cost private schools being advertised as English-medium – the whole curriculum is taught in English. Government schools usually only teach English as a subject from Class 5.[77] However, learning to read and write in English is typically by rote in low-cost private schools.

Three main interventions have been trialled and proven to be successful: that is reading and writing through a synthetic phonics approach, conversation via a package called Genki English and English pronunciation delivered through a computer and self-organising learning style[78] similar to that of the 'Hole in the Wall'[79] experiments. The 'Hole in the Wall' idea was devised by Sugata Mitra, then at NIIT Ltd, illustrating that children from a slum area were able to teach themselves computer skills using one computer between groups of children and a peer-learning approach which became known as self-organised learning. So how did these interventions turn out?

An alternative method for reading and writing, synthetic phonics, as well as improving conversational English through a programme called Genki English has been trialled in low-income areas of Delhi and Hyderabad. Early research in the UK has found that instruction using synthetic phonics benefits all pupils, including those whose first language is not English.[80] Compared to instruction using 'whole texts', a synthetic phonics programme has greater impact on reading and writing even for those from diverse non-English-speaking backgrounds.[81] The intervention in Hyderabad used the commercially available Jolly Phonics materials alongside lesson plans and workbooks specifically designed for the teachers and children in Indian low-cost private schools. After six months of lessons the findings showed a statistically significant higher achievement from the learning group over and above the control group who experienced their own traditional English lessons. This higher achievement occurred in reading, spelling and the ability to sound out letters as well as to blend words. The results showed that children from families, often with illiterate parents even in their mother tongue, being taught though a synthetic phonics model are able to blend and decode English words.[82]

In Delhi findings also replicated those in Hyderabad, where after a synthetic phonics intervention lasting a year those in the learning group outperformed those in the control group when using multilevel modelling to analyse test scores.[83] Not only is it that children show improvements in learning outcomes, but children show a great improvement in confidence and enjoyment of lessons. Teachers also change their teaching techniques owing to the training they receive alongside the lesson plans and the materials they are using, thus bringing greater teaching satisfaction. The conversational side also showed positive results, not only comparing achievement scores for treatment children compared to non-treatment but also concerning confidence with and the enjoyment of conversational English. In Hyderabad the pronunciation programme using computer technology in addition to peer-group pedagogy showed great improvements in the children's intonation and articulation of English.

It would seem worthwhile for international aid agencies to build upon the success of such programmes already trialled in low-income private schools in India and to consider other curriculum developments and trials, which should be researched rigorously.

It is suggested that aid agencies could help with curricula and pedagogy, not by providing free teacher training or free materials, but by helping develop low-cost resources, workbooks and teacher lesson plans around those interventions that have proven to be successful. Where programmes have been successful and school owners and parents are made aware of that success then private school entrepreneurs can make their own decisions regarding buying into it or not. They can only do this if the programme is affordable. Too much aid money has been wasted giving teacher training and materials for free, such as in the District Primary Education Project and with SSA. Billions of dollars of aid has been spent without any evidence of raising children's attainment or teacher enthusiasm or participation. Free materials often end up unused in school cupboards. Those materials that are actually bought will be much more likely to be utilised because they become a valued set of resources.

One other area that requires investigating in this regard is the Indian public examination system, which focuses on rote learning and memorisation. Only when these examinations change or a nationally or internationally recognised alternative is offered will the pedagogy move on substantially and in a meaningful way from rote learning.

STRENGTHENING LOW-COST PRIVATE SCHOOL FEDERATIONS

Some private school owners have, in India and Africa, organised themselves into federations or associations in order mainly to protect themselves from the threat of closure from government. Very little research has been carried out with regard to federations; however, some research from the city of Hyderabad, Andhra Pradesh, show there to be at least eight federations in operation. These include the Dynamic Federation of Private Schools, Deccan Federation of Private schools, Superb Federation of Private Schools and the Federation of Private Schools' Management. Not all low-cost private schools belong to federations; those who do not belong regard there to be no advantage of membership. However, one advantage of being within a federation is being able to replicate membership of a chain, without the school owner having to give up any control. Typically schools have to pay a membership fee to be part of the federation and this in some cases is used as a chit fund for members to borrow (in some cases without interest) when required. The Dynamic Federation collects Rs. 2000–3000 ($36–54) per month, per member which they put in a 'loans pot' to be distributed in a chit fund for members. According to Section 2(b) of the Chit Funds Act, 1982:

> Chit means a transaction whether called chit, chit fund, chitty, kuri or by any other name by or under which a person enters into an agreement with a specified number of persons that every one of them shall subscribe a certain sum of money (or a certain quantity of grain instead) by way of periodical installments over a definite period and that each such subscriber shall, in his turn, as determined by lot or by auction or by tender or in such other manner as may be specified in the chit agreement, he entitled to the prize amount.[84]

Chit funds in this case are a kind of unorganised scheme conducted between members to provide access to credit to improve one's school facilities. Without property rights, collateral or the ability to show profit levels this has been a successful way, although limited, for schools to access capital.

Federations also try to provide members with greater powers to address the harassment of government officials. More schools working in unification are more likely to be listened to by government when trying to speed up activities in certain departments. Events throughout the year are often organised by member schools so that pupils can come together for interschool sports events, science fairs and other competitions. Some federations produce their own support documents for curriculum development and help each other in longitudinal planning, including teacher training.

As indicated, not all schools see the benefit of belonging to a federation owing to the politics involved, with potential 'in-fighting' between school owners and the domination and favouritism of certain schools.

Low-cost private school federations also exist in other developing countries, such as Nigeria. In Lagos state, where there is an estimated 12,098 private schools, 74 per cent of which are 'unapproved', 56 per cent belong to federations or private school associations. Again the main reason for membership is to 'defend common interests and deter government action to close down private schools'.[85] Low-cost private school membership has also been seen to protect members against attack, not only from government but also elite private schools. The two main associations in Lagos state are the Association for Formidable Educational Development (AFED) and the National Association of Proprietors of Private Schools (NAPPS). In total, 2961 low-cost private schools are members of AFED, 2679 more elite private schools are members of NAPPS and around 1000 schools belong to smaller federations or associations such as the League of Muslim School Proprietors.

One way that international aid agencies could assist low-cost private schools is to use the federations and associations that already exist to support, develop and provide improvements and inputs. These could include:

- teacher training;
- the development of the curriculum;
- improvements in pedagogy;
- the provision of loans to improve facilities;
- the extension of philanthropy and scholarships;
- management training;
- providing information to parents in order for them to make better choices; and
- coordinating with government to maintain better knowledge and links.

Trying to strengthen federations and associations and building their capacity to provide sustainable inputs for their members, as well as improve the quality for children and parents, is one grass-roots method that should be investigated.

THE GRANTING OF PROPERTY RIGHTS

Without deeds to one's property or business it is difficult to gain access to capital. The threat of confiscation of the property and closure is always present. Hernando De Soto's famous work on property rights shows that without these rights and proof of ownership the poor are locked out of benefitting from capitalism and the ability to produce capital. Accordingly the poor possess assets but:

they hold these resources in defective forms: houses built on land whose ownership rights are not adequately recorded, unincorporated businesses with undefined liability, industries located where financiers and investors cannot see them. Because the rights to these possessions are not adequately documented, these assets cannot readily be turned into capital, cannot be traded outside of narrow local circles where people know and trust each other, cannot be used as collateral for a loan, and cannot be used as a share against an investment.[86]

If dwellings are built illegally without rights, the risks of demolition as well as paying steep fines or imprisonment are very real for the poor. However, lawfully gaining the rights to land can take decades in developing countries. Even when property rights are issued, knowing they will remain legal in the future is difficult, 'in fact, in every country we investigated, we found that it is very nearly as difficult to *stay* legal as it is to *become* legal'.[87] Hernando de Soto discovered that in Peru it took 289 days to legally register a business (working at it six hours a day) and the cost of legal registration was 31 times the monthly minimum salary. To gain legal authorisation to build a house on state land it took 6 years and 11 months, taking 207 steps with 52 government offices. In other developing countries it took even longer. For example, in Egypt to legally build a house could take between 6 and 11 years, in the Philippines 13 to 25 years and in Haiti, 19 years.[88] Owing to the stringent regulations, the number of steps to acquire legality and the cost associated with it, many of the poor living in developing countries become 'extra legal':

> Their only alternative is to live and work outside the official law, using their own informally binding arrangements to protect and mobilize their assets. These arrangements result from a combination of rules selectively borrowed from the official legal system, ad hoc improvisations, and customs brought from their places of origin or locally devised. They are held together by a social contract that is upheld by a community as a whole and enforced by authorities the community has selected. These extralegal social contracts have created a vibrant but undercapitalized sector, the centre of the world of the poor.[89]

The poor in developing countries are typically 'locked out of the capitalized economy by discriminatory laws'.[90] Buildings and land that are not legally owned cannot be used as collateral to raise loans. Houses and buildings that do not have legal title are 'mere shelter'[91] and therefore cannot be turned into 'live capital'. Only when the qualities of the property in terms of its economic and social usefulness are put down in writing via a title, contract or other record can it be regarded as live capital.

It could be difficult for aid agencies to assist in the granting of property rights to the low-cost private school entrepreneurs, as it is rather a political challenge requiring work on national legal systems. National governments need to recognise that the poor are not the problem, but the solution. The poor are only missing a legally integrated property system that is able to 'convert their work and savings into capital'.[92] Some kind of advocacy or dissemination of ideas with regard to legal property could be approached.

THE IDENTIFICATION OF HIGH ABILITY STUDENTS

Earlier research in India controlled for pupils' innate ability and background when comparing student outcomes and the impact different school management types make on achievement. Although a very raw and basic method of testing was used through the 'Standard Progressive Matrices Test' the data revealed some very high scoring children living in the slums and low-income areas of India. Simultaneously, but only anecdotally during this earlier research, it was observed that many children, including some of those identified with high scores, were set apart by the school owner or teacher, described as 'too active', 'not able to concentrate' or even 'very dull'. Such children appeared not willing to go along with their classmates engaged in chanting and rote-learning of material which it seemed they could easily master. This appeared to resonate with findings that gifted children may underachieve in schooling contexts that do not nurture their particular abilities.[93] Informal observations also show that pupil age is the primary determinant of grade – although certainly there are some observations of instances where children were informally identified as 'bright' or 'fast learners' and accelerated by one or two grades. Conversely, children informally identified as 'dull' or 'slow learners' were held back in the same way.[94] Research should be carried out in this area to systematically investigate whether these 'disruptive' children, or indeed any of their classmates, are intellectually gifted. The issues around 'identification' are critical. If gifted children are not being recognised in poor areas of developing countries then their talents are likely to end up being wasted. This is a disaster in terms of prosperity, both for the individuals concerned and for the societies in which they live, where such talents are likely to be in short supply. A child with the capacity to become a doctor, economist, scientist or engineer may end up repairing bicycle tyres at the roadside, owing to the lack of identification, nurturing and support.[95] Such students are not likely to have access to the educational stimulus they crave, leading to boredom and in some cases dropping out of education altogether.[96] Even in situations where there are 'talent searches', it is often the case that economically disadvantaged students find these difficult to access and are grossly under-represented.[97]

There is specific literature regarding disadvantaged gifted children in developed countries. Some believe that being disadvantaged and gifted implies a high practical intelligence associated with the ability to cope with the stresses associated with poverty – economic, educational and social.[98] The cultural context for the identification and support of high ability children seems also significant. Definitions of gifted children vary according to culture and these definitions are often underpinned by educational philosophies.[99] Steven Pfeiffer contends that the giftedness is a social construction, not something real; the construct always reflects what a given society deems culturally valued.[100] So any intervention of identification and nurturing should be sensitive to the cultural variations of what is conceptualised as giftedness and how such giftedness is viewed by school managers, teachers, parents and the students themselves. For example, Wu's work identifies how giftedness in Western societies is often interpreted through platonic notions of innate ability. By contrast, Chinese society with its philosophical roots in Confucianism suggests that giftedness is a consequence of hard work and perseverance.[101] C.A. Taylor also highlights the point that in countries where the priority is universal education, 'providing education to the great mass of average learners', supporting and nurturing the gifted receives little attention.[102] Some research has been conducted to develop a culturally relevant instrument to identify gifted black students in South Africa and to produce an assessment battery to select black South African students who could participate in a gifted programme.[103]

Apart from school, one crucial social environment for children is their family unit. This might have some effect on children from poor areas.[104] In fact, there is 'strong evidence that no matter what the initial characteristics (or gifts) of the individuals, unless there is a long and intensive process of encouragement, nurturance, education and training, the individuals will not attain extreme levels of capability in these particular fields'.[105]

Steven Pfeiffer and Tania Jarosewich point to a possible solution with their teacher rating scale, The Gifted Rating Scale-School Form (GRS-S) accurately identified high ability African American, Asian American, Hispanic and White children equally well in their large-scale, cross-cultural study: 'GRS-S appears to be less highly culturally loaded and works equally well across different racial/ethnic groups makes it an attractive gifted screening tool'.[106] Gifted disadvantaged children also require a teacher who can become a role model and whom they can come to respect.[107]

Gifted children also need to be provided with the ability to communicate with other gifted students in order for them to gain stimulation and focus. Even in the USA, 'a disproportionate number of potentially gifted children of color, economic disadvantage, or both, are not "adequately" provided for'.[108] Gifted summer academies are often a powerful antidote for intellectually precocious students who have had little or no academic challenge and minimal interaction with intellectual peers.[109]

It is suggested here that aid agencies could provide funding to investigate the identification and nurturing of high ability (intellectually gifted) children in poor and low-income and slum areas of India. It is estimated that this could make a substantial addition to the current literature and research and increase the contribution these children could make to their communities. Not only should identification procedures be investigated, but the supporting or provision of different nurturing possibilities should be considered. These could include the setting up of academies to support high ability children, and indeed illustrate to low-cost private school entrepreneurs and federations how this could be done within a market-driven system. The running of these academies for high ability students again could be on a for-profit basis, making them sustainable and run by those at the grass roots.

Funding could help to investigate the following:

(1) Currently, how, if at all, do those working in schools in the slum area of India, such as Shahdara, respond to gifted and talented children once identified? (Types of responses are likely to include being accelerated through grades, given extension work, or being ignored.)

(2) Is a school's response to gifted and talented children affected by their gender or any cultural or traditional aspects?

(3) Is it possible to create a viable and cost-effective 'summer academy programme' that can support and nurture gifted and talented children in poor communities? (The summer school programme is likely to use technology such as an online gifted academy, peer-learning, and mentor methods.)

(4) Is it possible to set out and run a viable and cost-effective summer academy programme for children identified as gifted and talented?

(5) Is there a residual impact to the summer academy? (That is, after the students complete the summer academy experience and return to their home, school and community what durable and continuing changes in attitude, knowledge, skill and/or academic-related behaviours persist?)

(6)   Is it possible for a full-time academy to be run profitably for high ability and gifted students by a federation in order to support pupils from their schools thus identified?

Funding would lead to a sustainable and scalable model for the identification, nurturing and support of high ability, gifted and talented children who would in turn assist those in their own communities, as Steven Pfeiffer puts it:

> A gifted student demonstrates uncanny high potential and a thirst to excel in one or more specific culturally valued academic domains. And a gifted student is likely to benefit from special educational programs, especially if they align with their unique profile of abilities and interests. We, of course, hope that our schools have the resources to include as many students of uncanny high potential and thirst to excel as possible, so that ultimately, from those who we select and from those who participate in gifted programs, a large percentage go on to accomplish extraordinary things.[110]

Extraordinary things happen in slum areas. The identification and nurturing of gifted students should become one of them.

CONCLUDING REMARKS

If aid agencies are to focus on the low-cost private schools' market they need to ensure their emphasis is not only at the grass roots, but what is initiated or contributed to is sustainable, improving both access and quality effectively and efficiently. This chapter has set out examples of where funding and expertise could be placed, allowing aid agencies and funding to minimise interference to the market mechanism but maximising impact for students, parents and schools. Strengthening what already exists by adding expertise, knowledge and technology along with the ability to disseminate good practice needs to be considered whatever the intervention may be. Good research, including randomised control trials, can again provide more information with regard who benefits most and why from interventions, allowing better targeting and the effective spending of aid. All strands of the process are crucial for the sustainable continuation of successful initiatives by the Indian government once aid agencies retract funding. If making markets work for the poor in education is to gain ground with the Indian government and national policy-makers, international aid now needs to show how best to strengthen and expand the sector.

NOTES

1. See, for example, http://www.mmw4p.org/dyn/bds/docs/detail/474/6.
2. Ferrand et al. (2004), p. 2.
3. Ibid., p. 24.
4. Riddell (2008), p. 408.
5. Paine (1791), p. 338.
6. Mill (1959 [1992]), p. 106.
7. Friedman and Friedman (1980), p. 185.
8. Ibid., p. 194.
9. Seldon (1986), p. 15.
10. Bettinger et al. (2009).
11. See, for example, Gallego (2002, 2004); and Sapelli (2003).
12. See for example Hsieh and Urquiola (2006).
13. Hoxby (2003).
14. Malik (2010), p. 23.
15. See http://www.edchoice.org/School-Choice/School-Choice-Programs.aspx; and Forster (2011).
16. Aud (2007).
17. Forster (2011).
18. Greene (2001).
19. Howell and Peterson (2002), p. 173; Forster (2011), p. 7.
20. Witte et al. (2008).
21. Wolf (2008).
22. Forster (2011), p. 12.
23. Sahlgren (2010).
24. Ibid.
25. Böhlmark and Lindahl (2012).
26. Shafiq (2010), p. 36.
27. See Nambissan and Ball (2010).
28. http://siteresources.worldbank.org/EDUCATION/Resources/278200-1121703274255/1439264-1178054414297/karthikmuralidharan.pdf pages1–2.
29. Hanlon et al. (2010).
30. Ibid., p. 1.
31. Ibid., p. 9.
32. Riddell (2008), p. 406.
33. Ibid., p. 407.
34. Ibid.
35. Hanlon et al. (2010), p. 48.
36. Ibid., p. 56.
37. Ibid., p. 41.
38. Barrera-Osorio (2007).
39. Hanlon et al. (2010), p. 61.
40. Ibid., p. 62.
41. Fiszbein and Schady (2009), p. xii.
42. Ibid.
43. Ibid., p. 3.
44. Behrman et al. (2000).
45. Ponce and Bedi (2008).
46. Behrman et al. (2005).
47. Reimers et al. (2006), p. 40.
48. Fiszbein and Schady (2009), p. 21.
49. Ibid., p. 24.
50. Ibid., p. 143.
51. Reimers et al. (2006), p. 39.

52. Ibid., p. 47.
53. Dias and Silva (2008).
54. Garg (2011).
55. Ibid.
56. Edify Annual Report 2011, http://www.edify.org/annual-report-2011.
57. Dixon (2003).
58. Ibid.
59. Ibid., p. 218.
60. See de Soto (2000).
61. See http://spontaneousorder.in/path-breaking-rules-under-the-right-to-education-act-in-gujarat/.
62. Fielden and LaRocque (2008), pp. 4–5.
63. Shah, http://spontaneousorder.in/path-breaking-rules-under-the-right-to-education-act-in-gujarat/.
64. http://www.graymatterscap.com/affordable-private-school-initiative/projects/school-ratings-project.
65. http://www.sef.org.pk/speip.asp.
66. Elacqua et al. (2011b).
67. McMeekin (2003); Wohlstetter et al. (2004); and Symonds (2000).
68. Brown et al. (2004); Steifel et al. (2000).
69. Foley (2010).
70. Elacqua et al. (2011a, 2011b).
71. Elacqua (2007).
72. Elacqua et al. (2011a).
73. Elacqua et al. (2011b), p. 8.
74. Ibid., p. 11.
75. Ibid., p. 12.
76. http://www.pearson.com/media-1/announcements/?i=1558.
77. Tooley and Dixon (2003).
78. Mitra et al. (2003).
79. Mitra (2003).
80. Linklater et al. (2009); Stuart (1999, 2004).
81. Stuart (1999, 2004).
82. Dixon et al. (2011).
83. Dixon and Schagen (2011).
84. Chit Funds Act, 1982, Financial Intelligence Unit, http://fiuindia.gov.in/relatedacts-chitfunds.htm.
85. Härmä (2011), p. 11.
86. de Soto (2000), p. 6.
87. Ibid., p. 21.
88. Ibid., pp. 20–8.
89. Ibid.
90. Ibid., p. 30.
91. Ibid., p. 50.
92. Ibid., p. 227.
93. McCoach and Siegle (2003).
94. Colangelo et al. (2004), p. 6.
95. Pfeiffer (2008, 2012).
96. Saul (1999).
97. Olszewski-Kubilius (2004); Pfeiffer (2003).
98. Sternberg and Arroyo (2006); Luthar (1999); Luthar et al. (2000); Maitra (2006).
99. Pfeiffer and Herman (2012).
100. Ibid.
101. Wu (2005).
102. Taylor (1993), p. 836.

103.   Tlale (1990); Skuy et al. (1990).
104.   Haywood and Mac and Ghaill (1998).
105.   Bloom (1985), p. 3.
106.   Pfeiffer and Jarosewich (2007), p. 47.
107.   Maree (2006).
108.   Pfeiffer (2003), p. 165.
109.   Olszewski-Kubilius (2004); Pfeiffer and Herman (2012).
110.   Pfeiffer (2012), p. 6.

5 Only the closed mind is certain

The accepted wisdom is that the poor need free government schools to educate them. This accepted wisdom is misguided. As discussed in Chapter 1, whether it was in nineteenth-century India and England, or, as set out in Chapter 3, in the slums and low-income areas of developing countries in the twenty-first century, Searchers, that is individual private school entrepreneurs, have been working silently out of the spotlight to educate the poor. No government or aid agency was needed, just parents being parents wanting choices and a better future for their children. That is all it took. Poor parents are no different from any other. The miracle of the market took over. As evidence shows, in India, as in other developing countries, low-cost private schools are providing an education for low-income families. Children gain better achievement levels and enjoy better facilities and smaller class sizes than in the government alternative. The poor have not been sitting around waiting for public education reforms to rid state schools of corruption, inefficiencies, or absent and idle teachers; they are abandoning public education and using private schools instead.

However, some regard this as a bad thing. Seemingly knowing more than the parents, the Planners believe this rational move is causing inequalities for the poorest that are left to acquiesce in failing government schools that now, according to some, resemble ghettos.[1] So the answer is to 'fix' the state sector for those that are left. Simple. All it should take is a few million dollars more of bilateral and multilateral aid in addition to national government funds and hopefully one day, although up to now it has not been possible, it will be put right. Once it is, the others will clamour back. A low-cost private school is no substitute, they say, for a well run, free and equal public one.

It is not what parents want. They have not got time for the state sector to be fixed, even if it ever could be; their children need educating now. In rural India 24 per cent of children are enrolled in private schools and in some states this figure exceeds 40 per cent.[2] In the poor urban areas where census data are available 65 per cent or more of children are attending low-cost private schools. Private school teachers are much more likely to be in school and teaching, even though they get paid in some cases four or five times less than government schoolteachers. The private sector is a burgeoning and vibrant one dismissed by some development experts and Planners as schools of last resort, offering 'little cause for optimism'.[3] Here is the reality, like it or not, low-cost private schools are hard to ignore and they are not going away. Parents have voted with their feet, illustrating people power and the miracle of the market at its finest. Parents do not know who Jeffrey Sachs is. They do not read UNESCO reports. They live in their own reality and time.

Low-cost private schools have now been around for a while. Almost 20 years ago Harold Alderman et al. found the majority of children in Lahore attending private schools, similarly in Haryana almost 15 years ago Yash Aggarwal discovered that more than half of the children were attending PUA schools there. Since then the sector has burgeoned even more and has now attracted the attention of aid agencies, donors, philanthropists and investors, in part owing to my work at Newcastle University.

International aid agencies need to show more power for every buck they spend. Meeting the Millennium Development Goal targets is just around the corner. With demands for increased international aid by developed country governments, showing that spending is making a difference to the lives of the poor is vital. However, it can only be a closed mind that would suggest continually pouring water into a bucket full of holes. Increased investments in government schools, according to Pratham and others, have been 'poorly' spent in India, with education outcomes showing no sign of improvement. International aid given to improve and develop government schooling is yet to 'translate into children acquiring basic abilities in reading and arithmetic'.[4]

Hence, low-cost private schools, a success story in their own right, might just be a good place to show some worthy and life-changing results utilising international aid. This would be a first for aid agencies with regard to targeting the private rather than the government sector in education. Is this a good move? Will it benefit the market, the school entrepreneurs, the parents, the teachers and, most of all, the children?

Some believe that aid can do more harm than good.

The misdirection and misappropriation of aid money would seem to suggest that aid could be channelled in a more productive way than it is currently. It seems odd that in a world where central planning has been shown to be inadequate it is still acceptable for aid to be allocated by Planners. As discussed in Chapter 2, Planners neither have the knowledge nor the ability to allocate resources to those who require it in the necessary quantities. Aid agencies have become lazy thinkers, showing a resistance to knowledge.[5] According to William Easterly and others it is now time to focus on the world's poor and how they would 'determine their own fate by their own home-grown institutions and initiatives'.[6] Research is of the utmost importance too. Monitoring and evaluating projects should be a *sine qua non*. Evaluating aid interventions using randomised control trials provides a scientific method dispelling 'wishful thinking, politically motivated conclusions, and pseudoscience',[7] which have dominated aid allocations thus far. The poor must to be consulted when aid is being allocated, until now they have been missed out of the equation. Hardly a surprise. As Brian Snowdon puts it:

> The intended customers of the aid industry are the poor people in developing countries. Unfortunately they have little or no voice! They have no voice in their own government, never mind having any kind of voice with the aid donors.[8]

Maybe now is the time for all that to change. Radical reforms are required to alter the way aid money is directed and transferred to the poor. If aid money is not directed at sustainable and scalable projects which focus on local entrepreneurs where communities are able to maintain the momentum once the aid has dried up, throwing good money after bad for the sake of it will perpetuate the ineffective, and sometimes damaging, consequences of aid. When aid agencies walk away, others need to be able to pick up the baton and run with it. The poor themselves are the solution. As Hernando De Soto puts it:

> The words 'international poverty' too easily bring to mind images of destitute beggars sleeping on the curbs of Calcutta and hungry African children starving on the sand. These scenes are of course real, and millions of our fellow human beings demand and deserve help. Nevertheless, the grimmest picture of the Third World is not the most accurate. Worse, it draws attention away from the arduous achievements of those small entrepreneurs who have triumphed over every imaginable obstacle to create the greater part of the wealth of their society. A truer image would depict a man and woman who have painstakingly saved to construct a house for themselves and their children and who are creating enterprises where nobody imagined they could be built. I resent the characterisation of such heroic entrepreneurs as contributors to the problem of global poverty. They are not the problem. They are the solution.[9]

So back to the original question.

'Can international aid successfully target the low-cost private schools' space in India and other developing countries without causing damage to the market that already exists?'

Possibly. But there is a warning that has been a thread throughout the book.

First, as set out in Chapter 1, there was the crowding out of indigenous education in nineteenth-century India by the British. Looking back through the history of schooling in India shows government interference has in the past destroyed flourishing markets in schooling, even if in the first instance this was not the intention. As Gandhi revealed at Chatham House:

> [t]he British administrators, when they came to India, instead of taking hold of things as they were, began to root them out. They scratched the soil and began to look at the root, and left the root like that, and the beautiful tree perished.[10]

In 1822 Sir Thomas Munro only set out to collect information regarding the education landscape in India. He made it perfectly clear that it was to be left to people to manage their own schools in their own way without any interference from the British. In fact Munro's teams found that the amount of education being provided without any state intervention was comparable at the time to that of Europe. Irrespective of the survey and census findings, the indigenous system was fated when in 1835 Thomas Babington Macaulay called for the setting up of publically funded village schools. Twenty years later the commencement of the demise of the indigenous schools began, which were to be brought under state control.

Second, survey and census data show that by 1861 almost every child in England, over 2.5 million of them, was in school, with the majority paying fees in schools not supported by the state. In 1851 only 15 per cent of schools received some kind of funding, even minimal, from the state. In 1870, initiated in the education Act, the introduction of Board Schools was supposed to fill gaps left by the already successful and prolific private schools and learning institutions. But everything changed. The desire to maximise control and budgets by the education bureaus resulted in the setting up of more Board Schools than was required. These schools crowded out the private ones as they were able to charge lower fees, supported by a new property tax now being paid by parents who, with this extra cost, could no longer afford private education tuition.

Third, in more recent times the provision of funding through bilateral and multilateral aid seems to have perpetuated failing government education systems rather than improving them. Again, even though there are moral, political and economic justifications for rich countries helping poor ones, corruption, waste, mismanagement and misappropriation of funds is a big problem. India's government school system is dominated by teachers who belong to strong teacher unions enjoying leverage with prominent political parties. Teachers are also substantially represented in parliament.[11] This makes the dismissal of a teacher almost impossible. Wages have been raised to levels where very little is left to spend on the children themselves.[12] Teacher activity in government schools is poor. Days are lost when teachers participate in union and political activities. In some cases government schools are closed for days on end; in schools that are open, children are virtually ignored.[13]

Even though the initial actions by governments were possibly based on good intentions, what in each case started out with recommendations to avoid at all costs interference in the original system, 'which prospers so well of itself',[14] ended up in the total destruction of what was working for and by the poor. Competition and the entrepreneur are the driving forces of the market process. 'Our discussions of entrepreneurship and competition have taught us that market process is always entrepreneurial, and that the entrepreneurial process is always competitive'.[15] Any government intervention that interferes with the market process, upsetting it by providing signals to entrepreneurs and consumers that do not reflect the true market position, could damage the low-cost private schools' market. Orderly markets depend upon the dis-orderliness of the entrepreneur. Planners have no place in an entrepreneurial process that is not predictable. Entrepreneurial activity is a procedure of discovery. If it were predictable and computable there would be no profit potential.[16] Care not to upset the workings of the market is imperative; if aid is to help rather than hinder low-cost private schools, maintaining the market mechanism as it is now (or somehow improving information within the market) must be of the utmost importance. Government officials and bureaus with vested interests should also be made to stand well clear.

Empirical evidence from around the world has been considered which suggests some alternative strategies for international aid agencies that could radically improve the effectiveness, efficiency, targeting and administration of international aid. According to the UK National Audit Office, fraud and corruption present a risk to the reputation of aid agencies, such as DfID, who are unable to provide a 'clear picture of the extent, nature and impact of leakage'[17] from their aid giving. On the 2010 Corruption Perceptions Index, which lists 178 countries scoring between 10 for 'highly clean' and 0 indicating 'highly corrupt' India appears 87th with a poor score of 3.3.[18] If aid is going to make a difference to the lives of the poorest then it needs to be directed at the grass-roots level to minimise waste, corruption and theft. It is suggested here that channelling any aid to India should therefore be through reputable NGOs or microfinance banks that have a proven track record in India. Such organisations could include Absolute Return for Kids, Pratham, Gray Matters Capital or the Indian School Finance Company. That way funds are more likely to reach those for whom they are intended.

Aid could target three main areas, highlighted by actors in the low-cost private school environment, which could be beneficial. However, treating schooling just as any other business operating in a market is crucial. Over the past decade of researching low-cost private schools these areas have stood out as ones where international aid could be focused: access, quality and information. Chapter 4 looked at each of these proposals in depth, utilising examples and evidence to support the proposition, so a relatively short summing up is provided here.

EXPANDING ACCESS

Even though a large proportion of parents are sending their children to low-cost private schools, there are still some parents who cannot afford the fees or the opportunity costs of taking their children away from an activity that benefits the household. Some parents might not want choice, but the small-scale voucher pilots that have been carried out already in India illustrate that many do. These projects, ENABLE and APRESt, could be built upon, and their frameworks used to improve operations and logistics. Evidence regarding the effects of vouchers specifically in the India context using RCTs should also be investigated further. Vouchers need to be targeted. There would be no benefit in providing everyone with a voucher; parents who can afford to send their children to low-cost private schools are already doing so. Targeting households below a predetermined income level whose children are currently either out of school or in government schools would be one solution. What has seemed to work successfully in India is the actual giving of a physical voucher to the parent to take and spend in an empanelled low-cost private school of their choice. The voucher, containing biometric information and barcodes, is used by the school owner to claim back the child's school fees, utilising various technologies. The schools still remain accountable to the parents with vouchers and owing to the use of technology and non-government actors for the transfer and distribution of fees there is less opportunity for fraudulent claims.

Cash transfers are another option for expanding PUA school access. Utilising the research evidence from other contexts, the suggestion is that these could be unconditional. Interestingly, in 2003 Lord Meghnad Desai observed:

> We are giving 50 billion dollars of overseas aid. There are a billion poor people in the world. Why don't we just find the poor and give them one dollar a week and do nothing else. No questions asked. What they do with the money is not our concern. That would probably do more to relieve poverty than anything else.[19]

Agreed.

Unconditionality would mean no monitoring of the condition, and so would be less costly for the international aid agency and implementing partners. The poorest have been found to typically spend the additional income provided through cash transfers on food and health, followed by children's schooling. The most difficult tasks are setting the CT amount and determining the type of targeting instrument to be used in order to ensure the effectiveness of the programme as well as to minimise the associated administrative costs. It is suggested here that targeting could be similar to that for a voucher programme: individual household assessments utilising an evaluation and verification process of children's schooling and income levels. This would require the presentation of documents such as a BPL card as in the Enable voucher programme. Other targeting approaches are possible, such as self-selection, categorical or community based, and should be investigated. The sum of the CT needs to provide enough money so that parents have cash left over after the essentials have been paid for to send their children to low-cost private schools. Other elements that need to be addressed and researched include the pressures beneficiaries might face from community leaders or village elites wishing to redistribute cash received through the transfer.[20] One must not underestimate the importance of the implementation and project design and it may be necessary to experiment, innovate, learn and develop a CT delivery system that could work for the whole country.[21]

IMPROVING QUALITY

Private school entrepreneurs are continually in competition with other school providers. The majority of owners are continuously trying to improve their quality in terms of facilities in order to attract new parents as well as to retain old ones. Accessing capital to do so can be difficult because of an inability to provide collateral or evidence of profitability. Because low-cost private schools are primarily run as businesses, making profits, improving facilities and infrastructure should be through microfinance loan schemes and other market based capital solutions. Here, international aid agencies could help by encouraging governments to make regulations less stringent for microfinance companies and businesses to enter the market, encouraging an expansion of capital providers targeting low-cost private schools. This would bring about more competition within this area as more providers entered the market. Private school owners wanting to improve their schools could do so just as any other business, through accessing loans and paying more competitive interest rates on those loans. What is needed is easier access to loans.

Of course international agencies could provide money to microfinance companies such as the Indian School Finance Company or Opportunity International, currently working with low-cost private schools in Ghana. But interest rates would still need to be charged and loans paid back.

Improving what goes on in the classroom again needs to focus on the market rather than giving away something for free. Generally, low-cost private schools follow the national curriculum, leading to the state exams. This in itself leaves little room for innovativeness. Rote learning is the typical learning pedagogy because most of the exams require only memorisation. Small-scale interventions have been carried out in low-cost private schools in India, including the use of synthetic phonics and Genki English to help in reading, writing and conversational English. Technology and peer learning have been experimented with regarding the improvement of English pronunciation. International aid money can build upon such projects that prove to be successful on a small scale by helping develop affordable resources and materials so that private schools can buy into such methods if they themselves deem them worthy of introduction into their schools for their children. Informing the market of such success is important because in the long run only the market will deliver scalability and sustainability of such pedagogical interventions and innovations.

One new initiative that aid agencies could fund through an intervention and research project is the identification and nurturing of high ability students. Observations suggest that school entrepreneurs and teachers know very little about how to recognise children with high ability. Even if they did, the result would be for them to skip a grade and this would be based on the ability to memorise through rote learning. In order for these children to make big differences for and within their own communities, new ways of exploring methods for identification and nurturing could be one way forward; something that could be sustained and scaled by the private schools' federations if found to be successful.

INFORMATION PROBLEM

Currently government and state regulations regarding gaining recognition are flaunted by paying bribes. Flaunted because, not only are the regulations too stringent for the low-cost private school owners to abide by, but they often do not target elements that stimulate student outcomes. It is therefore difficult for parents to gain information regarding standards in different schools and for school owners to actually know how their schools are doing compared to others in the neighbourhood, or indeed the whole city or state. Parents do typically visit two or three schools before choosing, as well as asking neighbours where they send their children to school. However, one idea being trialled in Hyderabad is an affordable private evaluation programme run by Gray Matters Capital. Over 200 schools have already paid to have their schools assessed. The school receives a breakdown of results for their individual school along with a comparison with other schools that have been rated. Parents receive a report card informing them of how their school has achieved. International aid could be made available to allow more private assessment companies to enter the market and perhaps subsidise the cost of the evaluation until school owners accept this method of assessment as valuable.

Again branding is another way to relay information regarding quality to parents in order for them to make more informed decisions with regard to school choice. Low-cost chains of private schools are relatively rare, and therefore more research needs to be done to ascertain their validity and addition to the market.

Finally, strengthening the federations and associations of private school managers may be crucial to the sustainability and scalability of some of the projects suggested here. Their ability to relate to governments and policy-makers seems important in order to disseminate and advocate what the low-cost private schools' market is actually achieving. Training school entrepreneurs to be more capable for such a role could be beneficial, giving them ideas as to how federations could become a pivotal hub in improving quality, access and advocacy.

POSTSCRIPT

Whatever path aid agencies take, their actions must not negatively affect the benefits millions of children are currently gaining from attending low-cost private schools. And that worries me. As I finish this book I am about to travel to India again, as I have been doing since 2000, to be with the children and school owners I hold so dear. I am so fortunate to have had the opportunity to be instrumental in the research and interventions that have taken place over the last 12 years. When I go to a low-income area or slum in India I see all that is good there. People are not sitting around waiting for aid agencies or national governments to come to their aid. Instead the poor rely on the market – vibrant, burgeoning and innovative. Aid has not got these people to where they are today. They have done it for and by themselves, just like they did in the nineteenth century. Even so, I have tried to set out in this book, having listened and talked to the Cheetahs and the Searchers over the years, ideas they believe could bring some benefits to the market miracle that already exists and which they themselves cultivated. If aid agencies are going to intervene at all, it must be with the utmost care. The children are of paramount importance. Their smiles lift my spirit and give me reason for being. I am determined to give them voice. The evidence is clear. These children are desperate to learn. They want success and aspire to become all they can. The private schools are the catalyst here. Not aid agencies or governments. Smiles, miracles and markets are the valuable jewel in the crown of modern India's schooling system. Do not allow that to change.

NOTES

1. Woodhead et al. (2013, in press).
2. Pratham (2011).
3. UNESCO (2008).
4. PAISA (2011), p. 7.
5. Banerjee (2007).
6. Easterly (2008), p. 24.
7. Easterly (2008), p. 25; and Duflo and Kremer (2008).
8. Snowdon (2003), p. 72.
9. de Soto (2000), pp. 35–7.
10. Dharampal (1995), p. 6.
11. Kingdon and Muzammil (2009), p. 124.
12. Government of India (1985), p. 25.
13. Shiva Kumar et al. (2009).
14. Brougham (1835), quoted in West (1994), p. 173.
15. Kirzner (1973), pp. 102–3.
16. Hayek (1948 [1980]); and Mises (1949 [1996]).
17. National Audit Office, 2011, http://www.nao.org.uk/publications/1011/dfid_financial_management_rept.aspx.
18. http://www.transparency.org/policy_research/surveys_indices/cpi/2010/results.
19. Hanlon (2004), p. 375.
20. See, for example, Chaudhry (2010), on unconditional cash transfers in Viet Nam.
21. See Hulme and Moore (2010) and Alviar et al. (2010), for more examples and in-depth discussions on targeting.

Bibliography

Acemoglu, Daron and James Robinson (2012), *Why Nations Fail: The Origins of Power, Prosperity, and Poverty*, London: Profile Books Ltd.

Aggarwal, Yash (2000), *Public and Private Partnership in Primary Education in India: A Study of Unrecognised Schools in Haryana*, New Delhi: National Institute of Educational Planning and Administration.

Alderman, Harold, Peter Orazem, and Elizabeth M. Paterno (1996), *School Quality, School Cost and the Public/Private School Choices of Low-Income Households in Pakistan*, Working Paper Series on 'Impact Evaluation of Education Reforms', Paper No. 2, Washington, DC: World Bank.

Alderman, Harold, Peter Orazem, and Elizabeth M. Paterno (2001), 'School quality, school cost and the public/private school choices of low-income households in Pakistan', *Journal of Human Resources*, **36**, 304–26.

Altonji, Joseph G., Todd E. Elder, and Christopher R. Taber (2005), 'Selection on observed and unobserved variables: assessing the effectiveness of Catholic schools', *Journal of Political Economy*, **113** (1), 151–84.

Alviar, Carlos, Francisco Ayala, and Sudhanshu Handa (2010), 'Testing combined targeting systems for cash transfer programmes: the case of the CT-OVC programme in Kenya', in David Lawson, David Hulme, Imran Matin, and Karen Moore (eds), *What Works for the Poorest? Poverty Reduction Programmes for the World's Extreme Poor*, Warwickshire: Practical Action Publishing, pp. 97–114.

Andrabi, Tahir, Jishnu Das, and Asim Ijaz Khwaja (2008), 'A dime a day: the possibilities and limits of private schooling in Pakistan', *Comparative Education Review*, **52** (3), 329–55.

Andrabi, Tahir, N. Bau, Jishnu Das, and Asim Ijaz Khwaja (2010), 'Are bad public schools public "bads"? Test scores and civic values in public and private schools', Working Paper cited by permission from J. Das.

Andrabi, Tahir, Jishnu Das, Asim Ijaz Khwaja, Tara Vishwanath, Tristan Zajonc, and The LEAPS Team (2007), *PAKISTAN: Learning and Educational Achievements in Punjab Schools (LEAPS): Insights to Inform the Education Policy Debate*. Executive Summary, 20 February.

Angrist, Joshua, Eric Bettinger, Erik Bloom, Elizabeth King, and Michael Kremer (2002), 'Vouchers for private schooling in Colombia: evidence from a randomized natural experiment', *The American Economic Review*, 1535–58.

Arif, Ghulam Mohamad and Najam us Saquib (2003), 'Production of cognitive life skills in public, private and NGO schools in Pakistan', *Pakistan Development Review*, **42** (1), 1–28.

Asadullah, Mohammad Niaz (2009), 'Returns to private and public education in Bangladesh and Pakistan: a comparative analysis', *Journal of Asian Economics*, **20**, 77–86.

Aslam, Monazza (2007), 'The quality of school provision in Pakistan: are girls worse off?', Global Poverty Research Group Working Paper 066.

Aslam, Monazza (2009), 'The relative effectiveness of government and private schools in Pakistan: are girls worse off?' *Education Economics*, **17** (3), 329–54.

Aslam, Monazza and Geeta Kingdon (2007), 'What can teachers do to raise pupil achievement?', The Centre for the Study of African Economies Working Paper Series, Working Paper 273, 27 June, accessed at www.bepress.com/csae/paper273.

Aud, Susan (2007), *Education by the Numbers: The Fiscal Effect of School Choice Programs, 1990–2006*, Indianapolis, IN: Friedman Foundation for Educational Choice, April.

Ayittey, George B.N. (2005), *Africa Unchained: The Blueprint for Africa's Future*, New York: Palgrave MacMillan.

Azam, Mehtabul, Aimee Chin, and Nishith Prakash (2010), 'The returns to English-language skills in India', CReAM Discussion Papers, No. 02-10, University College London.

Banerjee, Abhijit (2007), *Making Aid Work*, Cambridge, MA: MIT Press.

Banerjee, Abhijit and Esther Duflo (2006), 'Addressing absence', *Journal of Economic Perspectives*, **20** (1), 117–32.

Barnard, John, Constantine Frangakis, Jennifer Hill, and Donald Rubin (2003), 'Principal stratification approach to broken randomised experiments: a case study of school choice vouchers in New York City', *Journal of the American Statistical Association*, **98** (462), 299–323.

Barrera-Osorio, Felipe (2007), 'The impact of private provision of public education: empirical evidence from Bogota's concession schools', Policy Research Working Paper Series 4121, Washington, DC: The World Bank.

Barrera-Osorio, Felipe, Harry Anthony Patrinos, and Quentin Wodon (eds) (2009), *Emerging Evidence on Vouchers and Faith Based Providers in Education: Case Studies from Africa, Latin America and Asia*, Washington, DC: The World Bank.

Barrera-Osorio, Felipe, Marianne Bertrand, Leigh L. Linden, and Francisco Perez-Calle (2008), 'Conditional cash transfers in education: design features, peer and sibling effects evidence from a randomized experiment in Colombia', Working Paper Series 13890, NBER Working Paper Series.

Bauer, Peter T. (1976), *Dissent on Development*, revised ed., Cambridge, MA: Harvard University, Press.

Behrman, Jere R., Susan W. Parker, and Petra E. Todd (2005), 'Long term impacts of the Oportunidades Conditional Cash Transfer Program on rural youth in Mexico', Discussion Paper 122, Göttingen, Germany: Ibero-America Institute for Economic Research.

Behrman, Jere R., Piyali Sengupta, and Petra Todd (2000), 'The impact of PROGRESA on achievement test scores in the first year', Unpublished manuscript, Washington, DC: International Food Policy Research Institute.

Bettinger, Eric, Michael Kremer, and Juan E. Saavedra (2009), 'Education vouchers in Colombia', in Felipe Barrera-Osorio, Harry Patrinos, and Quentin Wodon (eds), *Emerging Evidence on Vouchers and Faith Based Providers in Education: Case Studies from Africa, Latin America, and Asia*, Washington, DC: The World Bank, pp. 71–7.

Bloom, Benjamin Samuel (ed.) (1985), *Developing Talent in Young People*, New York: Ballantine Books.

Böhlmark, Anders and Mikael Lindahl (2012), 'Independent schools and long-run educational outcomes: evidence from Sweden's large scale voucher reform', IZA Discussion Paper No. 6683.

Boone, Peter (1995), 'Politics and the effectiveness of foreign aid', NBER Working Paper 5308, October 1995.

Brandt, Willy (1980), *North-South: A Program for Survival (The Brandt Report)*, Cambridge, MA: MIT Press.

Brown, Heath, Jeffrey Henig, Natalie Lacireno-Paquet, and Thomas T. Holyoke (2004), 'Scale of operations and locus of control in market-versus mission oriented charter schools', *Social Science Quarterly*, **85**, 1035–51.

Census of India (2001), *Primary Census Abstract: Andhra Pradesh, Karnataka and Lakshadweep* (CD-Rom), New Delhi: Office of the Registrar General.

Chakrabarti, Rajashri and Paul E. Peterson (eds) (2008), *School Choice International: Exploring Public Private Partnerships*, Cambridge, MA: MIT Press.

Chaudhry, Peter (2010), 'Unconditional cash transfers to the very poor in central Viet Nam: is it enough to "just give them the cash"?', in David Lawson, David Hulme, Imran Matin, and Karen Moore (eds), *What*

Works for the Poorest? Poverty Reduction Programmes for the World's Extreme Poor, Warwickshire: Practical Action Publishing, pp. 169–78.

Chenery, Hollis B. (1964), 'Objectives and criteria of foreign assistance', in G. Ranis (ed.), *The United States and the Developing Economies*, New York: W.W. Norton.

Colangelo, Nicholas, Susan G. Assouline, and Muraca U.M. Gross (2004), *A Nation Deceived: How Schools Hold Back America's Brightest Students*, Iowa City: University of Iowa.

Colclough, Christopher and Anuradha De (2010), 'The impact of aid on education policy in India', DfID Recoup Working Paper No. 27.

Colclough, Christopher with Keith Lewin (1993), *Educating all the Children: Strategies for Primary Schooling in the South*, Oxford: Clarendon Press.

Collier, Paul (2007), *The Bottom Billion: Why the Poorest Countries are Failing and What Can be Done About it*, Oxford: Oxford University Press.

Commons Select Committee (2011), 'The future of DfID's programme in India', March, accessed at www.publications.parliament.uk/pa/cm201011/cmselect/cmintdev/writev/616/m07.htm

Cowen, Joshua (2008), 'School choice as latent variable: estimating the "complier average causal effect" of vouchers in Charlotte', *Policy Studies Journal*, **36** (2), 301–15.

Das, Jishnu and Tristan Zajonc (2010), 'India shining and Bharat drowning: comparing two Indian states to the worldwide distribution in mathematics achievement', *Journal of Development Economics*, **92**, 175–87.

Das, Jishnu, Priyanka Pandey, and Tristan Zajonc (2006), 'Learning levels and gaps in Pakistan', World Bank Policy Research Working Paper No. 4067.

De, Anuradha, M. Majumdar, Meera Samson, and C. Noronha (2002), 'Private schools and universal elementary education', in R. Govinda (ed.), *India Education Report: A Profile of Basic Education*, Oxford and New Delhi: Oxford University Press, pp. 131–50.

De, Anuradha, Reetika Khera, Meera Samson, and A.K. Shiva Kumar (2011), *PROBE Revisited: A Report on Elementary Education in India*, New Delhi: Oxford University Press.

DfID (2011), *UK Aid: Changing Lives, Delivering Results*, London: DfID.

Dharampal (1995), *The Beautiful Tree: Indigenous Indian Education in the Eighteenth Century*, Coimbatore: Keerthi Publishing House.

Dias, Magda Nucia Albuquerque and Maria do Rosario de Fatima e Silva (2008), *A Condicao de Pobreza das Familias Beneficiarias do Programa Bolsa Familia no Municipio de Bacabal – MA: a Importancia do Beneficio*, Brasilia: UNDP International Poverty Centre, accessed at

Biblioteca Virtual do Bolsa Familia, www.ipc-undp.org/publications/mds/34P.pdf.

Dixon, Pauline (2003), 'The regulation of private schools for low-income families in Andhra Pradesh, India: an Austrian economic approach', Unpublished PhD thesis, Newcastle University.

Dixon, Pauline and Ian Schagen (2011), 'Multilevel analysis of ARK Delhi Aspire data: final analysis', Unpublished report, Newcastle University.

Dixon, Pauline and James Tooley (2009), 'Private and public schooling in Mahbubnagar, Andhra Pradesh, India: a census and comparative survey', Working Paper, Newcastle University.

Dixon, Pauline, Ian Schagen, and Paul Seedhouse (2011), 'The impact of an intervention on children's reading and spelling ability in low-income schools in India', *School Effectiveness and School Improvement*, **22** (4), 461–82.

Dixon, Pauline, James Tooley, and S.V. Gomathi (2009), 'Private and public schooling in Mahbubnagar, Andhra Pradesh, India: a census and comparative survey', Working Paper, Newcastle University.

Dollar, David and Aart Kraay (2002), 'Growth is good for the poor', *Journal of Economic Growth*, **7**, 195–225.

Dollar, David and Aart Kraay (2004), 'Trade, growth, and poverty', *The Economic Journal*, (February) F22–F49.

Duflo, Esther and Abhijit Banerjee (2006), 'Addressing Absence', *Journal of Economic Perspectives*, **20** (1), 117–32.

Duflo, Esther and Rema Hanna (2005), 'Monitoring works: getting teachers to come to school', Mimeo, Massachusetts Institute of Technology.

Duflo, Esther and Michael Kremer (2008), 'Use of randomization in the evaluation of development effectiveness', in William Easterly (ed.), *Reinventing Foreign Aid*, Cambridge, MA: MIT Press, pp. 93–120.

Easterly, William (2006), *The White Man's Burden: Why the West's Efforts to Aid the Rest have Done so Much Ill and so Little Good*, London: Penguin.

Easterly, William (ed.) (2008), *Reinventing Foreign Aid*, Cambridge, MA: MIT Press.

Easterly, William (2009), 'Can the west save Africa?' *Journal of Economic Literature*, **47** (2), 373–447.

Elacqua, Gregory (2007), 'The politics of education reform in Chile: when ideology trumps evidence', paper presented at the Latin American Studies Association Annual Conference, Montreal, Canada, August 2007.

Elacqua, Gregory, Dante Contreras, Felipe Salazar, and Humberto Santos (2011a), 'The effectiveness of private school franchises in Chile's national voucher program', *School Effectiveness and School Improvement*, **22** (3), 237–63.

Elacqua, Gregory, Dante Contreras, Felipe Salazar, and Humberto Santos (2011b), 'Private school chains in Chile – do better schools scale up?' *Policy Analysis*, 16 August, No. 682, CATO Institute.

Enlow, Robert C. and Lenore T. Ealy (2006), *Liberty and Learning: Milton Friedman's Voucher Idea at Fifty*, Washington, DC: CATO Institute.

Ferrand, David, Alan Gibson, and Hugh Scott (2004), *Making Markets Work for the Poor – An Objective and an Approach for Governments and Development Agencies*, Woodmead, South Africa: ComMark Trust.

Fielden, John and Norman LaRocque (2008), *The Evolving Regulatory Context for Private Education in Emerging Economies*, Washington, DC: World Bank.

Fiszbein, Ariel and Norbet Schady (2009), *Conditional Cash Transfers Reducing Present and Future Poverty*, Washington, DC: The World Bank.

Foley, Eileen (2010), 'Approaches of Bill and Melinda Gates Foundation-funded intermediary organizations to structuring and supporting small high schools in New York City', accessed at www.eric.ed.gov/PDFS/ED510236.pdf.

Forster, Greg (2008), 'Vouchers and school choice: the evidence', *Economic Affairs*, **28** (2), 42–7.

Forster, Greg (2011), *A Win-Win Solution – The Empirical Evidence on School Vouchers*, Indianapolis, IN: The Foundation for Educational Choice.

French, Rob and Geeta Kingdon (2010), 'The relative effectiveness of private and government schools in rural India: evidence from ASER data', DoQSS Working Paper No. 10-03. Department of Quantitative Social Science, Institute of Education, University of London.

Friedman, Milton (1955), 'The role of government in education', in Robert A. Solo (ed.), *Economics and the Public Interest*, New Brunswick, NJ: Rutgers University Press, pp. 123–44.

Friedman, Milton (1958), 'Foreign economic aid: means and objectives', *Yale Review*, **47**, 501–16.

Friedman, Milton (1962), *Capitalism and Freedom*. Chicago, IL: University of Chicago Press.

Friedman, Milton (2005), 'Education, the next 50 years', *American Spectator*, **38** (9).

Friedman, Milton and Rose Friedman (1980), *Free To Choose*, Harmondsworth: Pelican Books.

Gallego, Francisco (2002), 'Competencia y Resultados Educativos. Teoria y Evidencia para Chile', *Cuadernos de Economia*, **39** (118), 309–813.

Gallego, Francisco (2004), *School Choice, Incentives, and Academic Outcomes: Evidence from Chile*, Cambridge, MA: Massachusetts Institute of Technology.

Garg, Nupur (2011), 'Low cost private education in India: challenges and way forward', Unpublished Masters' Thesis, Cambridge, MA: MIT Press.

Gauri, Varun and Ayesha Vawda (2003), 'Vouchers for basic education in developing countries: a principal-agent perspective', Policy Research Working Paper, Washington, DC: The World Bank.

Government of Andhra Pradesh (1999), *Vision 2020*, Hyderabad: Government of Andhra Pradesh.

Government of India (1985), 'Constituent Assembly (CA) Debates', Vol. IX, Official Report, New Delhi: Lok Sabha Secretariat, Government of India (Reprint), accessed at http://164.100.24.209/newls/constituent/vol9p13a.html.

Government of India (2005), 'Labour bureau, statistics, minimum wages', accessed 10 October 2005 at http://labourbureau.nic.in/wagetab.htm.

Govinda, R. (2005), 'An argument for School Based Management', paper presented at the Second National Learning Conference – Autonomous and Accountable Teacher for Quality Education, Bangalore, 22–24 October.

Goyal, Sangeeta (2009), 'Inside the house of learning: the relative performance of public and private schools in Orissa', *Education Economics*, **17** (3), 315 27.

Goyal, Sangeeta and Priyanka Pandey (2009), 'How do government and private schools differ? Findings from two large Indian states', South Asia Human Development, Report No. 30, Washington, DC: World Bank.

Greene, Jay (2001), 'Vouchers in Charlotte', *Education Next*, **1** (2), accessed at http://educationnext.org/vouchersincharlotte/.

Greene, Jay, Paul Peterson, and Du Jiangtao (1998), 'School choice in Milwaukee: a randomized experiment', in Paul Peterson and Bryan Hassel (eds), *Learning from School Choice*, Washington, DC: Brookings Institution, pp. 335–56.

Grey, Edward (2010), *The Travels of Pietro Dellan Valle in India*, New York: Cambridge University Press.

Hanlon, Joseph (2004), 'It is possible to just give money to the poor', *Development and Change*, **35** (2), 375–83.

Hanlon, Joseph, Armando Barrientos, and David Hulme (2010), *Just Give Money to the Poor: The Development Revolution from the Global South*, Virginia: Kumarian Press.

Härmä, Joanna (2009), 'Can choice promote education for all? Evidence from growth in private primary schooling in India', *Compare: A Journal of Comparative and International Education*, **39** (2), 151 65.

Härmä, Joanna (2011), *Education Sector Support Programme in Nigeria (ESSPIN): Logos Private School Census 2010–2011 Report – Report Number: LG 501*, UKAID (Dfid) and ESSPIN Nigeria, accessed at www.esspin.org.

Hartwell, Ronald M. (1995), *A History of the Mont Pelerin Society*, Indianapolis, IN: Liberty Fund.

Hayek, F.A. (1944), *The Road to Serfdom*, London: Institute of Economic Affairs.

Hayek, F.A. (1945), 'The use of knowledge in society', *The American Economic Review*, **35** (4), 519–30.

Hayek, F.A. (1948 [1980]), *Individualism and Economic Order*, Chicago, IL: University of Chicago Press.

Hayek, F.A. (1960), *The Constitution of Liberty*, Chicago, IL: University of Chicago Press.

Haywood, Chris and Máirtín Mac an Ghaill (1998), 'Gendered relations beyond the curriculum: peer groups, family and work', in A. Clark and E. Millard (eds), *Gender in the Secondary Curriculum*. London: Routledge, pp. 213–225.

Hill, Sam and Thomas Chalaux (2011), 'Improving access and quality in the Indian education system', OECD Economics Department Working Papers, No. 885, OECD Publishing, accessed at http://dx.doi.org/10.1787/5kg83k687ng7-en.

Howell, William G. and Paul E. Peterson (2002), *The Education Gap: Vouchers and Urban Schools*, Washington, DC: Brookings Institution Press.

Hoxby, Caroline M. (2003), 'School choice and school competition: evidence from the United States', *Swedish Economic Policy Review*, **10**, 11–67.

Hsieh, Chang-Tai and Miguel Urquiola (2006), 'The effects of generalized school choice on achievement and stratification: evidence from Chile's voucher program', *Journal of Public Economics*, **90**, 1477–503.

Hulme, David and Karen Moore (2010), 'Assisting the poorest in Bangladesh: learning from BRAC's "Targeting the Ultra Poor" programme', in David Lawson, David Hulme, Imran Matin, and Karen Moore (eds), *What Works for the Poorest? Poverty Reduction Programmes for the World's Extreme Poor*, Warwickshire: Practical Action Publishing, pp. 149–68.

Johnson, Craig and Michael T. Bowles (2010), 'Making the grade? Private education in northern India', *Journal of Development Studies*, **46** (3), 485–505.

Johnson, Harry G. (1962), *Money, Trade and Economic Growth: Survey Lectures in Economic Theory*, London: George Allen and Unwin.

Joshi, Shruti (2008), 'Private budget schools in Hyderabad City, India: a reconnaissance study', Atlanta, Georgia: Gray Matters Capital, Working Paper series, accessed at www.graymatterscap.com.

Kakwani, Nanak, Fábio Veras Soares, and Hyun H. Son (2005), 'Conditional cash transfers in African countries', Working Paper No. 9, United Nations Development Programme.

Keefer, Philip and Stuti Khemani (2004), 'Why do the poor receive poor service?' *Economic and Political Weekly*, 935–43.

Khan, Shahrukh R. and David M. Kiefer (2007), 'Educational production functions for rural Pakistan: a comparative institutional analysis', *Education Economics*, **15** (3), 327–42.

Kingdon, Geeta (1996), 'Student achievement and teacher pay', Discussion Paper No. 74, STICERD, London School of Economics, August.

Kingdon, Geeta and J. Drèze (1998), 'Biases in educational statistics', *The Hindu*, 6 March.

Kingdon, Geeta and Mohd Muzammil (2009), 'A political economy of education in India: the case of Uttar Pradesh', *Oxford Development Studies*, **37** (2), 123–44.

Kingdon, Geeta and Francis Teal (2010), 'Teacher unions, teacher pay and student performance in India: a pupil fixed effects approach', *Journal of Development Economics*, **91**, 278–88.

Kirzner, I.M. (1973), *Competition and Entrepreneurship*, Chicago, IL: University of Chicago Press.

Kremer, Michael, Nazmul Chaudhury, F. Halsey Rogers, Karthik Mularidharan, and Jeffrey Hammer (2005), 'Teacher absence in India: a snapshot', *Journal of the European Economic Association*, **3** (2–3), 658–67.

Kremer, Michael, Nazmul Chaudhury, Jeffrey Hammer, Karthik Muralidharan, and F. Halsey Rogers (2004), 'Teacher and health care provider absence: a multi country study', Mimeo, World Bank.

Kremer, Michael, Karthik Mularidharan, Nazmul Chaudhury, Jeffrey Hammer, and F. Halsey Rogers (2004), *Teacher Absence in India*, accessed October 2004 at http://siteresources.worldbank.org/DEC/Resources/36660_Teacher_absence_in_India_EEA_9_15_04_-_South_Asia_session_version.pdf.

Kremer, Michael, Karthik Muralidharan, Nazmul Chaudhury, Jeffrey Hammer and F. Halsey Rogers (2006), 'Missing in action: teachers and health workers absence in developing countries', *Journal of Economic Perspectives*, **20** (1), 91–116.

Krueger, Alan and Pei Zhu (2004), 'Another look at the New York City school voucher experiment', *American Behavioural Scientist*, **47** (5), 658–98.

Kunz, Diane B. (1997), 'The Marshall Plan reconsidered', *Foreign Affairs*, **76** (May–June), 162–70.

Ladd, Helen F. and Edward B. Fiske (2000), *School Choice in New Zealand: A Cautionary Tale*, Washington, DC: Brookings Institution.

Lewin, Keith M. (2007), 'Improving access, equity and transitions in education: creating a research agenda', Create, Research Monograph, No. 1, University of Sussex.

Linklater, Danielle L., Rollanda E. O'Connor, and Gregory J. Palardy (2009), 'Kindergarten literacy assessment of English only and English language learner students: an examination of the predictive validity of three phonemic awareness measures', *Journal of School Psychology*, **47**, 369–94.

Luthar, Suniya S. (1999), *Poverty and Children's Adjustment: Developmental Clinical Psychology and Psychiatry*, Thousand Oaks, CA: Sage.

Luthar, Suniya S., Dante Cicchetti, and Bronwyn Becker (2000), 'The construct of resilience: a critical evaluation and guidelines for future work', *Child Development*, **71**, 543–62.

Maitra, K. (2006), 'An Indian perspective on gifted education: the synergy of India', in B. Wallace and G. Eriksson (eds), *Diversity in Gifted Education: International Perspectives on Global Issues*, London and New York: Routledge, pp. 141–50.

Malik, Allah Bakhsh (2010), *Public Private Partnerships in Education: Lessons Learned from the Punjab Education Foundation*, Philippines: Asian Development Bank.

Maree, J.G. (2006), 'A fairer deal for the gifted disadvantaged in rural areas in South Africa', in B. Wallace and G. Eriksson (eds), *Diversity in Gifted Education: International Perspectives on Global Issues*, London and New York: Routledge, pp. 136–42.

McCoach, D. Betsy and Del Siegle (2003), 'Factors that differentiate underachieving gifted students from high-achieving gifted students', *Gifted Child Quarterly*, **47**, 144–54.

McMeekin, Robert (2003), 'Networks of schools', *Education Policy Analysis Archives*, (16), accessed at http://epaa.asu.edu/epaa/v11n16/.

Mehrotra, S. and P.R. Panchamukhi (2006), 'Private provision of elementary education in India: findings of a survey in eight states', *Compare*, **36** (4), 421–42.

Mehta, A.C. (2002), *Some Reflections on Sarva Shiksha Abhiyan*, New Delhi: NIEPA.

Metcalf, K.K. (1999), 'Evaluation of the Cleveland scholarship and tutoring program, 1996–1999', Unpublished manuscript, Indiana University.

Mill, J.S. (1959 [1992]), *On Liberty, and Other Writings*, Cambridge: Cambridge University Press.

Mises, Ludwig von (1949, [1996]), *Human Action: A Treatise on Economics*, 4th ed., San Francisco: Fox & Wilkes.

Mitra, Sugata (2003), 'Minimally invasive education: a progress report on the "hole-in-the-wall" experiments', *British Journal of Educational Technology*, **34** (3), 367–71.

Mitra, Sugata (2006), *The Hole in the Wall: Self-Organising Systems in Education*, New Delhi & New York: Tata-McGraw-Hill Pub.

Mitra, Sugata, James Tooley, Pari Inamdar, Pauline Dixon (2003), 'Improving English pronunciation: an automated instructional approach', *Information Technologies and International Development*, **1** (1), 75–84.

Mooij, Jos (2008), 'Primary education, teachers' professionalism and social class: about motivation and demotivation of government school teachers in India', *International Journal of Educational Development*, **28**, 508–23.

Mooij, Jos and Jennifer Jalal (forthcoming), 'Primary education in Delhi, Hyderabad and Kolkata: Governance by resignation, privatisation by default', in Stephanie Tawa Lama-Rewal and Joël Ruet (eds), *The Changing Governance of Indian Metropolises in the 2000s: A Comparative Sector Based Study*, Routledge: New Delhi.

Moyo, Dambisa (2010), *Dead Aid: Why Aid is not Working and How there is Another Way For Africa*, London: Penguin Books.

Muralidharan, Karthik and M. Kremer (2008), 'Public and private schools in rural India', in Rajashri Chakrabarti and Paul E. Peterson (eds), *School Choice International: Exploring Public Private Partnerships*, Cambridge, MA: MIT Press, pp. 91–110.

Nambissan, Geetha B. (2003), 'Educational deprivation and primary school provision: a study of providers in the city of Calcutta', IDS Working Paper 187, Institute of Development Studies.

Nambissan, Geetha B. and Stephen J. Ball (2010), 'Advocacy networks, choice and private schooling of the poor in India', *Global Networks*, **10** (3), 324–43.

Narayan, Krishna (2007), 'Innovative public management strategies to address the problems of teacher absenteeism and poor quality in rural government primary schools in India', A research paper in partial fulfilment of the requirements for obtaining the degree of Masters of Art in Development Studies, Institute of Social Studies, the Hague, 2007.

National Audit Office (2011), *Department for International Development: Financial Management Report: Report by the Comptroller and Auditor General HC 820 Session 2010–2012*, London: The Stationery Office, accessed at www.nao.org.uk/publications/1011/dfid_financial_management_rept.aspx.

NCERT (2009), *Learning Achievement of Class III Children, Mid-Term Assessment Survey Under SSA*, New Delhi: NCERT.

NCT (1986), *The Teacher and the Society – Report of the National Commission on Teachers – I, Controller of Publications*, New Delhi: Government of India.

Ohara, Yuki (2012), 'Examining the legitimacy of unrecognised low-fee private schools in India: comparing different perspectives', *Compare: A Journal of Comparative and International Education*, **42** (1), 69–90.

Olszewski-Kubilius, Paula (2004), 'Talent searches and accelerated programming for gifted students', in N. Colangelo, S.G. Assouline, and M.U.M. Gross (2004), *A Nation Deceived: How Schools Hold Back America's Brightest Students* (Volume II), Iowa City: University of Iowa, pp. 69–76.

Oosterbeek, Hessel, Juan Ponce, and Norbert Schady (2008), 'The impact of unconditional cash transfers on school enrollment: evidence from Ecuador', Policy Research Working Paper 4645, Washington, DC: World Bank.

Paine, Thomas (1791), *Rights of Man*, Chapter 5, Part II, in *The Thomas Paine Reader*, New York: Penguin, 1987.

PAISA (2011), *Do Schools Get Their Money?* Delhi, India: Accountability Initiative Centre for Policy Research.

Patrinos, Harry and Chris Sakellariou (2009), 'Returns to schooling and vouchers in Chile', in Felipe Barrera-Osorio, Harry Patrinos, and Quentin Wodon (eds), *Emerging Evidence on Vouchers and Faith Based Providers in Education: Case Studies from Africa, Latin America, and Asia.* Washington, DC: The World Bank, pp. 39–52.

Pearson, Lester B. (1969), *Partners in Development – Report of the Commission on International Development*, New York; Washington, DC and London: Praeger.

Peterson, Paul and William Howell (2004), 'Voucher research controversy', *Education Next*, Spring.

Pfeiffer, Steven (2003), 'Challenges and opportunities for students who are gifted: what the experts say', *Gifted Child Quarterly*, **47** (2), 161–9.

Pfeiffer, Steven (2008), *Handbook of Giftedness in Children*, New York: Springer.

Pfeiffer, Steven (2012), 'Lesson learned from working with high-ability students', *Gifted Education International*, 1–12.

Pfeiffer, Steven and K. Herman (2012), 'Engineering the future: a STEM-based summer academy for high ability students', Working Paper, Florida State University.

Pfeiffer, Steven and Tania Jarosewich (2007), 'The Gifted Rating Scales-School Form: an analysis of the standardisation sample based on age, gender, race and diagnostic efficiency', *Gifted Child Quarterly*, **51** (1), 39–50.

Ponce, Juan and Arjun S. Bedi (2008), 'The impact of a cash transfer program on cognitive achievement: the Bono de Desarrollo Humano of Educador', Discussion Paper 3658, Bonn, Germany: Institute for the Study of Labor.

Prahalad, C.K. (2005), *The Fortune at the Bottom of the Pyramid: Eradicating Poverty Through Profits, Enabling Dignity and Choice Through Markets*, New Jersey: Wharton School Publishing, Pearson.

Pratham (2011), *Annual Status of Education Report (Rural) 2010*, Provisional, Mumbai and New Delhi: Pratham Resource Centre.

Pratham (2012), *Annual Status of Education Report (Rural) 2011*, Provisional, Mumbai and New Delhi: Pratham Resource Centre, accessed at http://pratham.org/images/Aser-2011-report.pdf.

The Probe Team (1999), *Public Report on Basic Education in India*, Oxford and New Delhi: Oxford University Press.

Ramachandran, Vimala, Madhumita Pal, Sharada Jain, Sunil Shekhar and Jitendra Sharma (2005), *Teacher Motivation in India*, Brighton: Knowledge and Skills for Development Program, accessed at www.azimpremjifoundation.org.

Rana, Kumar, Abdur Rafique, and Amrita Sengupta (2002), *The Delivery of Primary Education: A Study in West Bengal*, Delhi: TLM Books and Pratichi (India) Trust

Rangaraju, Baladevan, James Tooley, and Pauline Dixon (2012), *The Private School Revolution in Bihar – Findings for a Survey in Patna Urban*, Delhi, India: India Institute.

Rawls, John (1971), *A Theory of Justice*, Cambridge, MA: The Belknap Press of Harvard University Press.

Reimers, Fernando, Carol De Shano da Silva, and Ernesto Trevino (2006), *Where is the 'Education' in Conditional Cash Transfers in Education?* Montreal: UNESCO.

Riddell, Roger (2008), *Does Foreign Aid Really Work?* Oxford: Oxford University Press.

Rose, Pauline (2002), 'Is the non-state education sector serving the needs of the poor?: Evidence from east and southern Africa', paper prepared for DfID seminar in preparation for the 2004 World Development Report.

Rouse, Cecilia (1998), 'Private school vouchers and student achievement', *Quarterly Journal of Economics*, **113** (2), 553–602.

Sachs, Jeffrey (2001), 'The strategic significance of global inequality', *The Washington Quarterly*, Summer, 187–98.

Sachs, Jeffrey (2005), *The End of Poverty: Economic Possibilities for Our Time*, London: Penguin, Allen Lane.

Sachs, Jeffrey (2008), *Common Wealth Economics for a Crowded Planet*, London: Penguin, Allen Lane.

Sahlgren, Gabriel H. (2010), 'Schooling for money: Swedish education reform and the role of the profit motif', IEA Discussion Paper No. 33, London: IEA.

Sapelli, Claudio (2003), 'The Chilean voucher system: some new results and research challenges', *Cuadernos de Economia*, **40** (121), 530–8.

Saul, Mark (1999), 'Kerosinka: an episode in the history of soviet mathematics', *Notices of the American Mathematical Society*, **46** (10), 1217–20.

Save the Children UK, South and Central Asia (2002), 'Private sector involvement in education: a perspective from Nepal and Pakistan', submission to 'The private sector as service provider and its role in implementing child rights', Office of the High Commissioner for Human Rights, Geneva, 20 September.

Seldon, Arthur (ed.) (1986), 'The riddle of the voucher: an inquiry into the obstacles to introducing choice and competition in state schools', Hobart Paper 21, London: IEA.

Shafiq, M. Najeeb (2010), 'Designing targeted educational voucher schemes for the poor in developing countries', *International Review of Education*, 56, 33–50, doi: 10.0117/s11159-009-9147-y.

Shiva Kumar, K., Anuradha De, Jean Drèze, Meera Samson, and Shyamshree Dasgupta (2009), '"Education for all" is the policy, but what is the reality?' *Frontline*, **26** (6), 14–27, accessed at www.frontline-onnet.com/fl2606/stories/20090327260608800.htm.

Skuy, Mervyn, Vanessa Gaydon, Sharon Hoffenberg, and Peter Fridjhon (1990), 'Predictors of performance of disadvantaged adolescents in a gifted program', *Gifted Child Quarterly*, **34**, 92–101.

Snowdon, Brian (2003), 'In search of the Holy Grail: William Easterly on the elusive quest for growth and development – an interview', *World Economics*, **4** (3), 51–92.

Snowdon, Brian (2005), 'A global compact to end poverty: Jeffrey Sachs on stabilisation, transition and weapons of mass salvation', *World Economics*, **6** (4), 11–68.

Snowdon, Brian (2007), *Globalisation, Development and Transition – Conversations with Eminent Economists*, Cheltenham, UK and Northampton, MA: Edward Elgar Publishing.

Snowdon, Brian (2009), 'The Solow Model, poverty traps, and the foreign aid debate', *History of Political Economy*, **41** (1), 241–62.

Soto de, Hernando (2000), *The Mystery of Capital: Why Capitalism Triumphs in the West and Fails Everywhere Else*, New York: Basic Books.

Steifel, Leanna, Robert Berne, Patrice Iatarola, and Norm Fruchter

(2000), 'High school size: effects on budgets and performance in New York City', *Educational Evaluation and Policy Analysis*, **22**, 27–39.

Sternberg, Robert J. and Carmen G. Arroyo (2006), 'Beyond expectations: a new view of the gifted disadvantaged', in B. Wallace and G. Eriksson (eds), *Diversity in Gifted Education: International Perspectives on Global Issues*, London and New York: Routledge, pp. 110–24.

Stuart, Morag (1999), 'Getting ready for reading: early phoneme awareness and phonics teaching improves reading and spelling in inner-city second language learners', *British Journal of Educational Psychology*, **69**, 587–605.

Stuart, Morag (2004), 'Getting ready for reading: a follow-up study of inner city second language learners at the end of Key Stage 1', *British Journal of Educational Psychology*, **74**, 15–36.

Symonds, William C. (2000), 'For-profit schools: they're spreading fast. Can private companies do a better job of educating America's kids?' *Business Week*, 7 February.

Taylor, C.A. (1993), 'Programs and practices for identifying and nurturing giftedness and talent in Africa', in K.A. Heller, F.J. Monks, and A.H. Passow (eds), *International Handbook of Research and Development of Giftedness and Talent*, Oxford, New York, Seoul, and Tokyo: Pergamon Press, pp. 833–48.

Tlale, Chimane D. (1990), 'Principles for the design of a culturally relevant instrument to identify gifted black secondary school children', Unpublished PhD thesis, Pretoria: University of Pretoria.

Tooley, James (2008), *E.G. West: Economic Liberalism and the Role of Government in Education – Continuum Library of Educational Thought, Volume 14*, London: Continuum.

Tooley, James and Pauline Dixon (2003), *Private Schools for the Poor: A Case Study from India*, Reading, UK: CfBT.

Tooley, James and Pauline Dixon (2005), 'Is there a conflict between commercial gain and concern for the poor? Evidence from private schools for the poor in India and Ghana', *Economic Affairs*, **25** (2), 20–6.

Tooley, James and Pauline Dixon (2007), 'Private schooling for low-income families: a census and comparative survey in East Delhi, India', *International Journal of Educational Development*, **27** (2), 205–19.

Tooley, James and James Stanfield (eds) (2003), 'Government failure: E.G. West on education', Occasional Paper 130, London: The Institute of Economic Affairs.

Tooley, James, Pauline Dixon, and S.V. Gomathi (2007), 'Private schools and the millennium development goal of universal primary education: a census and comparative survey in Hyderabad, India', *Oxford Review of Education*, **33** (5), 539–60.

Tooley, James, Pauline Dixon, and Olanrewaju Olaniyan (2005), 'Private and public schooling in low-income areas of Lagos State, Nigeria: a census and comparative survey', *International Journal of Educational Research*, **43**, 125–46.

Tooley, James, Yong Bao, Pauline Dixon, and John Merrifield (2011), 'School choice and academic performance: some evidence from developing countries', *Journal of School Choice: Research, Theory, and Reform*, **5** (1), 1–39.

Tooley, James, Pauline Dixon, Yarim Shamsan, and Ian Schagen (2010), 'The relative quality and cost-effectiveness of private and public schools for low-income families: a case study in a developing country', *School Effectiveness and School Improvement*, **21** (2), 117–44.

UN (2011), *The Millennium Development Goals Report 2011*, New York: United Nations.

UNDP (2003), *Human Development Report 2003*, New York: United Nations Development Programme.

UNDP (2011), *Human Development Report 2011, Sustainability and Equity: A Better Future for All*, New York: United Nations Development Programme.

UNESCO (2008), *Overcoming Inequality: Why Governance Matters – EFA Global Monitoring Report, 2009*, Paris: UNESCO Publishing.

Venkatanarayana, M. (2004), 'Educational deprivation of children in Andhra Pradesh: levels and trends, disparities and associate factors', Working Paper 362, Centre for Development Studies, August, accessed at www.cds.edu.

Watkins, Kevin (2000), *The Oxfam Education Report*, Oxford: Oxfam GB.

Watkins, Kevin (2004), 'Private education and "education for all" – or how not to construct an evidence-based argument', *Economic Affairs*, **24** (4), 8–11.

Watkins, Kevin (2011), 'Universal primary education by 2015? Not without some innovative financing – the MDGs promised education for all, but to avoid failing the world's most disadvantaged children, we need a global fund', *The Guardian*, 28 December, accessed at www.guardian.co.uk/global-development/poverty-matters/2011/dec/28/universal-primary-education-innovative-financing.

West, Edwin G. (1965), *Education and the State: A Study in Political Economy*, London: Institute of Economic Affairs.

West, Edwin G. (1975), 'Education slowdown and public intervention in 19th century England: a study in the economics of bureaucracy', *Explorations in Economic History*, **12**, 61–87.

West, Edwin G. (1985), 'The demise of "free" education', Challenge, White Plains, NY: M.E. Sharpe Inc.

West, Edwin G. (1994), *Education and the State: A Study in Political Economy*, 3rd ed., Indianapolis, IN: Liberty Fund.

West, Edwin G. (1997), 'Educational vouchers in principle and practice: a survey', *World Bank Research Observer*, **12** (1), 83–103.

Witte, John F., Patrick J. Wolf, Josh M. Cowen, David J. Fleming, and Juanita Lucas-McLean (2008), 'MPCP longitudinal educational growth study baseline report', Education Working Paper Archive, Department of Education Reform, College of Education and Health Professions, University of Arkansas, 7 April, accessed at www.uark.edu/ua/der/EWPA/Research/School_Choice/1806.html.

Wohlstetter, Priscilla, Courtney L. Malloy, Guilbert C. Hentschke, and Joanna Smith (2004), 'Improving service delivery in education through collaboration: an exploratory study of the role of cross-sectoral alliances in the development and support of charter schools', *Social Science Quarterly*, **85**, 1078–96.

Wolf, Patrick (2008), 'School voucher programs: what the research says about parental school choice', *Brigham Young University Law Review*, **2008** (2), 415–46, accessed at http://lawreview.byu.edu/archives/2008/2/90WOLF.FIN.pdf.

Wolf, Patrick, Babette Gutmann, Michael Puma, Brian Kisida, Lou Rizzo, Nada Eissa, and Matthew Carr (2010), *Evaluation of the D.C. Opportunity Scholarship Program, Final Report*, US Department of Education, National Centre for Educational Evaluation and Regional Assistance Institute of Education Science.

Woodhead, Martin, Mel Frost, and Zoe James (2013, in press), 'Does growth in private schooling contribute to education for all? Evidence from a longitudinal, two cohort study in Andhra Pradesh, India'. *International Journal of Educational Development*, **33** (1).

World Bank (1997), 'Pakistan – towards a strategy for elementary education', Report No. 16670-PAK, Washington, DC: World Bank.

World Bank (2003), *Making Services Work for Poor People: World Development Report 2004*, New York: World Bank; Oxford University Press.

Wu, Echo H. (2005), 'Factors that contribute to talented performance: a theoretical model from a Chinese perspective', *Gifted Child Quarterly*, **49**, 231–46.

Young, G.M. (1957), *Macaulay, Prose and Poetry*, Cambridge, MA: Harvard University Press.

Index

Introductory Note: The letter 'n' in a page number refers to a note at the end of the chapter.